Success Skills Series

SHARON (

EFFECTIVE NETWORKING

HOW TO WIN IN THE BUSINESS DATING GAME

Published by Marshall Cavendish Business
An imprint of Marshall Cavendish International
1 New Industrial Road, Singapore 536196

Other Marshall Cavendish Offices
Marshall Cavendish Corporation. 99 White Plains Road, Tarrytown NY 10591-9001, USA • Marshall Cavendish International (Thailand) Co Ltd. 253 Asoke, 12th Flr, Sukhumvit 21 Road, Klongtoey Nua, Wattana, Bangkok 10110, Thailand • Marshall Cavendish (Malaysia) Sdn Bhd, Times Subang, Lot 46, Subang Hi-Tech Industrial Park, Batu Tiga, 40000 Shah Alam, Selangor Darul Ehsan, Malaysia.

Marshall Cavendish is a trademark of Times Publishing Limited

National Library Board, Singapore Cataloguing-in-Publication Data

Connolly, Sharon.
Effective networking : how to win in the business dating game / Sharon Connolly. – Singapore : Marshall Cavendish Business, c2013.
p. cm. – (STTS Success skills series)
Includes index.
ISBN : 978-981-4398-08-4 (pbk.)

1. Social networks. 2. Self-presentation.
I. Title. II. Success skills series (ST Training Solutions)

HM741
650.13— dc23   OCN823268453

Printed by Fabulous Printers Pte Ltd

ACKNOWLEDGEMENTS

I often wonder whether the audience reads the acknowledgements page. It has been my favourite page to write as it meant that I had finally completed the book, and can now thank the people who mean the most to me.

First, thanks to Mary Flavelle, the queen of networking, for introducing me to the business dating game. Mary, it's the book you spoke about writing for years. I've done it for both of us.

I'd like to acknowledge every LadiesWhoLatte leader. These girls give up their time and inspire thousands of women to achieve and succeed through their giving and support and mentoring. Ladies, you have no idea how much your support and encouragement means to your groups. Keep up the good work. Special thanks to Chris Carter, Alison Crook, Opheilia Messer, Sarah Ducker and Billie Sharp.

Thanks also to Shirley Taylor for being a great editor and supporter of me in Singapore.

It is said that you are the sum of the five people that you surround yourself with most often. If that's true, then I must be awesome and fabulous in many ways from the constant support of my seven 'Shenanigans Girls'! Love you all: Amanda Page, Angela Collette, Brooke Skeers, Gina Galvin, Jacqui Rankin, Jordana Brumby, Michelle Lewis.

Finally, this book is dedicated to Sean and Laura Connolly. If I can write and publish a book, then believe you can achieve anything that you want to, and I hope you are proud of your mum.

PREFACE

Congratulations on picking up this copy of *Effective Networking*. I'm very proud to include this in the STTS Training Success Skills series. This series includes several short, practical books on a range of topics that will help you develop your skills and enhance your success at work and in your personal life too.

The Success Skills series was originally created to meet the needs of participants of STTS Training public workshops. After attending our workshops, many participants expressed a real desire to continue learning, to find out more about the topic, to take it to another level. They were hungry for knowledge. Just the effect I hoped for when I set up STTS Training in 2007. With the Success Skills series of books, the experience and expertise of our trainers can be enjoyed by many more people.

As Series Editor, I've enjoyed working with the authors to make sure the books are easy-to-read, highly practical, and written in straightforward, simple language. Every book is packed with essential tools and strategies that will make you more effective and successful. We've included illustrations throughout that reinforce some key points, because I believe we learn more if we add some fun and humour. You'll also notice some key features that highlight important learning points:

Myth Buster Here you will find a statement that is not true, with notes on the true facts of the matter.

Fast Fact Useful snippets of information or special points to remember.

Aha! Moment

This is a 'light bulb' moment, when we note something you may be able to conclude from a discussion. Don't forget to note your own 'Aha! Moments' perhaps when you receive some extra insight that clarifies an important point.

Try This

Here you'll find a suggestion for how you can put a special point into practice, either at home or at work.

Danger Zone

You'll find some words of warning here, such as things to avoid or precautions to take.

Star Tips

At the end of each chapter you'll find a list of Star Tips — important notes to remind you about the key points.

By picking up this book you have already shown a desire to learn more. The solid advice and practical guidelines provided in this book will show you how you can really go from good to great!

Good luck!

Shirley Taylor

Shirley Taylor
Series Editor
CEO, STTS Training Pte Ltd

www.sttstraining.com
www.shirleytaylor.com

Your Steps to Success

Visit www.sttstraining.com now to download your free e-book **'Your 7 Steps to Success'** containing motivating advice from our Success Skills authors. You can also read lots of author articles and order the latest titles in the Success Skills series.

CONTENTS

INTRODUCTION

I started my own business as a computer skills trainer in 1993. I ran that business very successfully for 11 years until one morning I decided I didn't want to be an IT trainer any more. Despite everyone thinking I was completely nuts, I trained to be an image consultant. Then I found out that I had not really been running a business for 11 years! As an IT trainer, I had a handful of clients and I repeatedly ran courses for the same clients year after year. The odd one would disappear and then I'd send out a small mailshot and pick up another client, but I did nothing else to generate business.

After training as an image consultant, I soon realised there was more to running a business than turning up and delivering a training. For the most part, I saw each client just once. After I'd shown them colours, styles, make-up and taken them shopping, they didn't need me any more. If I was going to be successful, I quickly had to learn how to generate a constant flow of interest for my services, and turn that into a stream of paying customers who would then go on to refer me. I had no idea how to do that.

Advertising didn't work. It was also still very early days in terms of the Internet, so online promotion tools were not available to me either. I was at a loss. After doing a little research, I joined my local Chamber of Commerce and signed up for a 'Women in Business' group. And there I discovered networking.

My first event was a disaster. I was nervous and flustered when I left the house, and didn't notice my car was low on fuel. I ran out of petrol on the way and had to walk half a mile in heels to the petrol station and then back to refuel the car. I very nearly turned around and went back home, but I didn't. By the time I got to the event I was nearly an hour late, my feet were killing me, and I was stressed and flustered.

The speaker was David Blaine, and he talked about a disastrous and almost fatal round-the-world boat trip he had attempted after he had made and lost his first million. Thirty ladies sat listening, wide-eyed and open-mouthed as he spoke about the challenges he faced and how, despite catastrophic circumstances, he picked himself up and started again. He was the first of many inspiring speakers I have been privileged to meet while networking.

After the speaker, each lady stood up and gave a one-minute presentation about herself and her business. Many of them did it very badly, myself included! As the event finished, the organiser came over to greet me enthusiastically. This lady was Mary Flavelle. She introduced me to the power of networking, and without her I probably wouldn't have written this book. Mary is known as Berkshire's 'Queen of Networking' — she knows everyone and everyone knows her. She's an Irish firecracker. Mary taught us all how to network by example. She works a room effortlessly, takes care of everyone, and remembers the smallest detail about everyone she meets. Mary's job was to run networking events and get people to become members of the Chamber of Commerce.

I attended many of Mary's events and as many other networking events as I could. As I got better and better at it, clients soon materialised, and my business grew. Five years later I was a regular networker and speaker in my local areas. In fact, I became too busy to attend the lunches that used to bring me business. As a mum of two children, breakfast events were impossible, lunches took up too many hours of my day, and evening events were tricky. I approached my Chamber of Commerce and asked if they would be interested in holding networking coffee mornings at child-friendly times. They said no one would be interested in this type of event, so I started my own. I emailed all ladies in my address book and asked them to come for an informal coffee at Starbucks. My subject line read "Let's be LadiesWhoLatte". Just five women turned up to my first coffee morning, but it was great. Mary Flavelle was there and she asked if she could set up a similar group in her local Starbucks. Natalie Holiday also set up one in hers. They both invited their contact lists to an informal coffee morning.

Five years later, we have over 50 LadiesWhoLatte meetings across the world. Every month thousands of women meet, inspire and motivate each other over coffee. I have never charged anyone to attend a meeting.

I just felt passionately that networking was a great way for women to learn and grow their businesses. I know that my networking groups have been pivotal in the success of the businesses of many women.

Growing your business and developing yourself through networking is not a chore, it's a pleasure. I hope that by reading this book you can reap as many rewards as I have.

Sharon Connolly
www.sharonconnolly.com

ASSESS YOURSELF

1. You have to be confident to be a successful networker:

a) True

b) False

2. The main reason you should attend networking events is to:

a) Win new business.

b) Drink lots of wine.

c) Meet new people for social reasons.

d) Find new suppliers.

e) All of the above.

3. The best places to find networking opportunities are:

a) Events run by your local Chamber of Commerce.

b) Inside the company that you work for.

c) At sports and social clubs.

d) In coffee shops.

e) Singles nights run by dating organisations.

4. An elevator pitch is:

a) Something that makes you sound more impressive than you are.

b) A fine-tuned, practised introduction about yourself and your organisation.

c) A business proposal you give in the elevator on the way to the event.

5. It's best to attend a networking event:

a) Alone.

b) With colleagues so you can stick together. There is power in numbers!

c) Either is fine.

6. When attending a networking event you should bring:

a) Sales literature and examples of your products.

b) A supply of business cards.

c) Client testimonials.

d) Leaflets about forthcoming events.

7. Facebook is:

a) A complete waste of time.

b) A fun place to stalk past loves and laugh at how fat old school friends have become.

c) An essential tool for connecting with people you have met at networking events.

8. Networking can never take the place of traditional sales within a business:

a) True

b) False

9. When attending a networking event, you should wear:

a) Something that makes you stand out.

b) What you would normally wear to work.

c) What you would wear to a party.

d) It doesn't matter what you wear.

10. How long should you wait after an event to follow up with a new contact?

a) The next day.

b) A week.

c) A month.

d) A year.

e) Never.

Answers:

1. The answer is (b) False. You don't have to be confident to be a successful networker. Most people are very nervous when they start networking, or in any new situation. This book is packed with strategies to help you handle your nerves and use communication tools effectively. Even if you are not confident to begin with, you will soon become a very confident networker.

2. It really doesn't matter what you answered in question 2. The most important thing is to set specific networking goals so you know if you have been successful. Chapter 1 outlines many ways in which networking can add colour to your personal and professional life. Networking to meet new friends is a totally acceptable reason. Be specific about what you want to achieve with your networking, and evaluate your success regularly.

3. A skilled networker will look for opportunities everywhere — in a coffee shop, at the gym, within the family. New networkers should take every opportunity to practise their skills in places such as the coffee shop queue. The best place for you to network will depend on the types of people you want to meet and where these people gather. We will discuss more about this in Chapter 1.

4. I hope you answered (b). In Chapter 2 we look at the importance of having a number of pre-prepared introductions about yourself, and you'll also find out why it's called an elevator pitch.

5. The answer is (c). When you first start attending events it can be great to have business colleagues or friends with you for moral support. If all of you have the same objectives it can be really useful to have a team from your organisation there so as to meet the maximum amount of prospects. However, if you attend with colleagues from your organisation, standing and talking to them for the duration of the event will not be productive.

6. The best answer would be (b). You will learn that networking is about building relationships rather than selling. If you bombard someone with sales literature or sample products when you first meet them, you are not networking — you are selling. Networking events are where you engage people, and if relevant you can follow up afterwards with additional material. At some events it would be acceptable to promote your product, but tread carefully and create relationships first.

7. I hope you answered (c). If you don't use Facebook, you will be missing out on registration for many events that might help you network. Facebook is also a great platform for finding out more about others and contributing to groups. You can set your privacy settings so you decide what information people can see about you. In Chapter 8 we look at the many benefits of Facebook.

8. What did you answer? (a) is correct! Networking can never take the place of traditional sales. Cold calling and door-to-door selling is mind-numbingly boring. It's time-consuming and often ineffective. Networking is fun and effective.

9. You could have answered anything except (d). It really does matter what you wear to events. You need to be remembered and to stand out. If you normally wear stylish clothes to work, then of course it's fine to wear those when networking. If it's an evening networking event it's sometimes fine to be a little glamorous too. Chapter 5 is all about being memorable.

10. If you answered (a), (b) or (c), then you're on the right track. Follow up when you say you will follow up with someone. If you say you'll call them next week for a coffee, then make sure you call them next week for a coffee. Don't wait a year to get back in touch. Chapter 4 talks about identifying your 'Big Fish'. Prioritise your contact list and stay in contact with those who will help your network grow. Do try to find ways to make yourself more visible to everyone you meet though. Volunteering as a speaker or perhaps writing a blog may accomplish this.

THE NETWORKING LAUNCH PAD

"A good head and a good heart are always a formidable combination."

Nelson Mandela

If we are to take our networking seriously and get some real results, we need to create a strategic plan, measure our efforts, and record our successes and failures. In addition to incurring an economic cost, our networking will also have a great time cost, so we must make sure we get a return on investment.

In this chapter we will look at some of the reasons why you may benefit from networking. I will help you to define your ideal networking contacts and help you to think about where you might find these contacts.

Why network?

1. Networking to win more business

Networking is a brilliant way to win more business and to nurture existing business. As you progress through the chapters of this book, you will discover that you are unlikely to sell at networking events. However, if you are a smart networker, you can build relationships that will result in new business and referrals for new business.

At one of the ladies networking events that I ran, an aerobics instructor setting up a new class found that every participant in her class had come from networking. She attended the same networking event three months in a row, and her class became completely full. The ladies not only enjoyed the class, they also took this as another opportunity to network with each other for business.

 Fast Fact

Networking can be a viable alternative to expensive advertising or cold calling. Some companies get all of their customers from networking and referrals.

2. Networking to promote your personal or corporate brand

You may not have a product or service to sell, but you might attend a networking event to raise awareness about you as a person, or your company as a brand. This can be particularly powerful if your company is a sponsor for an event. Having your logo visible to all participants of the networking event can be very helpful. On one occasion I received a call from a potential client after a networking event that I didn't even attend. My name and job title were on the guest list, so the client called me after the event. He said that it was a really busy event and that he had tried to find me, but must have missed me. I did admit that I wasn't there, and we became strategic partners.

 Danger Zone

You do actually need to attend networking events to become successful. In the example above, I got lucky!

3. Networking to find suppliers

You may be networking to find new companies to use as suppliers. Through networking I have met my graphic designer, maintenance contractor, office space supplier, wine supplier and caterer. I met them, formed trusting relationships with them, and subsequently went on to hire them and recommend them to others.

 Myth Buster

Networking is not just for people looking for new business leads. As an influential networker, you will also be in a position to award business to other people.

4. Networking to find associates and strategic partners

Depending on your business, you may network to find people in similar or complementary businesses to yours. As a speaker and trainer, I have found it really useful to connect with other speakers and trainers. I've been hired by them, referred them to conference providers and also run collaborative workshops with some of them. I'd say that this has been the major source of my business over the last two years.

5. Networking for personal development

Many networking events have speakers — some good, some not so good — but I've had the privilege of listening to some great speakers at networking events. These speakers are often using networking as a platform to gain exposure to an audience that may subsequently hire or refer them. On many occasions I've heard world-class speakers share amazing information in a condensed format for less than the price of a meal.

 Fast Fact

You can save money, time and get a brilliant return on investment by attending personal development events held by organisations such as your local Chamber of Commerce.

6. Networking for social reasons

There are times when you might need to extend your social circle. When I had my first child, I needed to find like-minded mothers who also had new children so that I could share experiences and organise play-dates for my son. When I moved to Singapore, I didn't know anyone. Before I could even think about starting my business, I needed to find some friends to drink wine with to keep me sane. I needed to find people who could help me settle in to Singapore and share their local knowledge and expertise. I found them through networking.

When Katrina first arrived in Singapore, she plucked up the courage to join the Friday drinks night of my dragon boating club. She'd heard it was a great place to meet expatriates in Singapore. Within five minutes she knew where to get her hair cut, where to shop and which supermarkets delivered, and we introduced her to a great real estate agent who found her an ideal apartment three days later. I told Katrina about my monthly women's networking event, so she attended the next meeting and made even more great connections.

7. Networking to find a job

If you are looking for a new job, networking is a great way to put yourself in front of new potential employers, or perhaps recruitment consultants who will be able to help you.

Josie was a macrobiotic crop scientist who had recently relocated to Singapore with her husband. In case you don't live in Singapore, let me tell you we don't grow much here, so Josie was not optimistic about finding a job in Singapore in her area of expertise. At her first business networking event, she met Anna from Hong Kong. Anna was just tagging along with her friend who was a regular visitor to the group. She happened to work for a huge food manufacturer in Hong Kong and was looking for someone with Josie's skills to cover maternity leave for one of her staff. At one chance meeting over a glass of wine, Josie got a job and Anna fulfilled a contract.

8. Networking to grow in confidence

Networking can be a great way to help you combat shyness. You will have to introduce yourself to people and chat with them, and you may also have the opportunity to present. If this scares you to death, then networking can be a great way for you to build your confidence by taking baby steps.

At my first few networking events I was petrified at having to do a one-minute introduction of myself. However, the more I did it, the easier it became, until eventually I volunteered to give talks at networking events. Ten years later, I am travelling the world as a professional speaker.

9. Networking inside your organisation

Being an effective networker is a vital key to success inside many large organisations. You will need to create great relationships with key stakeholders and with external suppliers and clients. You need to stand up, stand out and get noticed so you are visible for opportunities that will help your career path.

10. Networking because you have been sent

This is not a great reason to go to a networking event. If your boss registers you to attend a networking event, you need to know his reason for this. What is the objective for you attending? If you don't know why you are going, then you cannot know if your networking has been successful. If your boss cannot tell you, then look through the reasons above and make one of them your personal goal.

 Fast Fact

When I educate people about their personal brand, I make them aware that no matter where they work, their most important contract of employment is with themselves. When you are working for an organisation, tell yourself that you are temporarily renting your employment services. Ultimately, you are responsible for your own personal development and continued growth. Take advantage of every opportunity that your employer gives you. If there is no benefit to your immediate job, then think about how this opportunity to network might help you if you were in another role in your organisation, or if you were looking for other opportunities in the future.

Setting your goals

As you read through the chapters of this book you will realise that effective networking requires planning, an investment in time, and often also a financial investment. It is important that you get a return on that investment (ROI). How will you know if your networking efforts are successful? You need to have a clear plan and set specific goals and objectives for your desired outcome. Only when you know precisely what you want to achieve will you be able to know if you have been successful. Take the time now to plan your networking objectives.

Try This

My main reasons for networking are:

_____

_____

My ideal networking contact is:

_____

_____

Who do you want to meet?

As an image consultant, my ideal networking client is a badly-dressed person coming up to me on the verge of tears, whimpering "Help me, please. I need to book every consultation you have and I need it tomorrow." Unfortunately, that has never happened, and it's probably unlikely to happen. Few of us are in a business where our clients will immediately buy what we have on offer, so let's look at how we can narrow down our ideal networking contacts.

Before we can identify the best contact for you, I need you to think a little bit more about 'you', about the product or service you are advertising, how are you packaging yourself and your offering, and who exactly would be interested.

It's important that you create a niche for yourself. This will make it easier for you to source and hone in on your target. Let's look at an example.

Michelle is a skilled life coach with several years' experience in coaching men and women to navigate obstacles in their career or personal lives. She's trained to coach anyone to overcome any challenges they may encounter. This is great, but it's not going to help her network.

Let's look at how Michelle might target people at different networking events.

Michelle attends a women's coffee morning. She knows that many of the women are mothers, having just dropped off their children at school. She knows that some of the older women may have recently retired, or are not currently working. Any working women are most probably working part-time, and in this sort of group there may be women who are thinking of starting their own businesses or turning a hobby into a business.

When Michelle is asked to introduce herself to the group, she could say:

> *"Hello, I'm Michelle and I'm a life coach. Whatever problems you are experiencing in your life, I can help you to overcome them."*

Everyone has problems, so this statement would apply to everyone — but no one would feel as if it directly applied to them.

Consider if she had said this instead:

> *"Hello, I'm Michelle and I'm a coach who specialises in work-life balance. The clients I like to work with most*

struggle to juggle being a mother and finding time to think about their career, or even find five minutes to sit and have a cup of tea! I've helped over 100 stressed mums to gain the confidence to start a new business, or go for a promotion at work, or just find balance in their lives. Do you know anyone who needs a fairy godmother like me?"

This is an elevator pitch, and I'll talk more about this in Chapter 3. This pitch from Michelle might not resonate with the whole audience, but there will be ladies sitting there thinking, "Wow! She is talking to me, she's describing my life — she could help me."

Michelle would often find that after chatting with some of the women they would ask, "Do you work with men as well?" or "Do you coach business start-ups?" Of course she would always answer "Yes", but by setting a niche for this meeting she would be more successful.

Let's now imagine that Michelle attends a networking event for lawyers. Again she can coach any of them through any obstacle, but she might choose to say:

"Hello, I'm Michelle and I specialise in helping lawyers become more confident when they are presenting evidence in court."

Any lawyer who is nervous when attending court will think, "Wow! She's talking directly to me."

I would advise Michelle to think about who she most enjoyed working with and then think about where she might find that type of client. If she said she enjoyed working with all clients, I would ask her to look back through her client records and find which type of client she received most revenue from in the past.

As an image consultant, I found that more than 70 per cent of my clients were professional business women aged 35–50 who either had their own businesses or worked in senior positions in large organisations. I have clients who are younger and older, and I also have male clients, as well as unemployed clients, but most of these actually come through as referrals from my target audience. So I've found that my best networking strategy is to network where I will find this niche of 35–50-year-old business women.

 Danger Zone

If you are not selling a product or service, don't think this does not apply to you. You might be looking to network with your next potential boss. Think about your dream job within your current organisation or perhaps a competitor — who do you need to meet for them to offer you that job opportunity, and where could you meet them?

Targeting your niche

Let's revisit the previous questions. First I'm going to ask you to write down your niche, your unique selling point and what you have to offer. Don't worry too much about the wording. This is not your elevator pitch. It's just a bit of self-discovery that you are putting on paper.

For example:

> *"I'm a talented marketing graduate looking for an entry level marketing job. I completed work experience in the IT industry and really enjoyed it. I want to work in a large company with lots of opportunities. I get really excited about new technologies, and know I would be passionate about creating marketing campaigns for edgy new products."*

Try This

Write down your niche.

_____

_____

Now think about who you would really like to meet.

For example:

> *My ideal networking contact would be the HR or marketing manager for a large IT company. I'd really love to work for Apple or Microsoft.*

Try This

Write down your ideal contact.

_____

_____

Finding the hip and happening events

So now you should be clear about what you want to get out of networking, what you have to offer and who you would like to meet. Let's now plan where to go. An Internet search on networking events in your local area should reveal a lot of opportunities, but here are some ideas.

1. Chambers of Commerce

You may have a local or regional Chamber of Commerce. Depending on where you live, there may also be additional groups for expat communities. Check their websites for the number of members they have and the type of events they hold. The people who attend Chamber of Commerce meetings will mostly be business people. I have found Chambers to be excellent for networking as well as personal development, as their functions can attract brilliant speakers and large crowds. I've often found that my Chamber of Commerce memberships included great additional benefits such as free legal advice.

2. Networking associations

There are many organisations specifically set up for networking and business sharing. BNI is a worldwide weekly breakfast meeting, LadiesWhoLatte is my networking women's organisation. The Athena Network is a global women's networking group.

3. Professional associations

If you are looking for business contacts in your field, the various professional associations are a good starting point. As a speaker, I go to Asia Professional Speakers Singapore. As an aspiring speaker, I may go to Toastmasters. As an image consultant, I could belong to the Association of Image Consultants International (AICI). Be aware that sometimes you'll be networking with your competitors, but I prefer to say "No competitors, only friends."

These associations will be good for professional development and forming strategic alliances. Allies in the same market may also often share details of great suppliers. Think about areas that may be complimentary to yours. As an image consultant I work closely with life coaches, so I sometimes go to International Coaching Federation (ICF) meetings. If my niche was female senior accountants, then it would be a good idea to find out where senior female accountants go. I might start my research by picking up some publications targeted at my audience and taking a look at events advertised there.

Most professional organisations will let you attend two meetings before you commit to join as a member, so try a few before you join.

No competitors. Only friends.

4. Sporting events

Don't underestimate this by any means. Many a multi-million dollar deal is hatched on a golf course. Professional people like to work hard and play hard. The dragon boating team that I belong to is full of professional high achievers. One of the team members, an independent financial advisor, is delighted to have over 30 of the 100 members as her clients, not to mention the referrals they pass on to her. She's my financial advisor, she recommended me, and I became a supplier for her organisation.

5. Informal gatherings

These include mother and baby groups, flower arranging, night classes, a friend's birthday party. If there are more than three of you there, I'd call it a networking opportunity.

6. Trade shows

These can be great fact-finding days. You'll discover a team of salespeople on their stands just wishing for someone to talk to. Go to trade shows where the companies you want to talk to will be exhibiting. Stop by their stand, chat with them and ask questions. You can find out the names of other people who work there and about potential opportunities within minutes. If you call the company, it's too easy for them to hang up on you or say they are busy. When you are standing in front of someone at their exhibition stand, they will be much more courteous.

But just because you *can* network in these places, it doesn't mean you necessarily *should* network there. Remember that you previously detailed your ideal networking clients, so think about where you are most likely to meet them. It's unlikely that you'll find the HR Director of Google at your flower arranging class.

 Try This

Do some research online if necessary, and compile a list of where you could network in your area.

Place a star by the events where you are most likely to meet your ideal client. These events will become the focus of your strategic networking plan.

Place a tick by the events where you would feel most comfortable. These events will be where you will hone your skills and practise the art of networking until you become a more confident networker.

7. Leverage your existing network

I currently have 650 Facebook friends, most of whom I do actually know. Facebook statistics say the average user has 130 friends. I'll be talking about networking via social media in a later chapter, but I want to take this opportunity to get you to think about who you already know. As you work through the chapters of this book and become more confident and expert at networking, bear in mind that you already have a vast network of friends, family, colleagues and aquaintances who can connect you to opportunities. Start thinking about who you know, who they might know and how you can make use of your current resources.

Star Tips when planning your networking

1. Set yourself clear goals. Understand why you are networking, and exactly what you want to achieve. You could have more than one goal. List them all.

2. Identify your niche. What is special about you or your organisation? Think about your unique offering and be clear about what makes you different.

3. Research online for networking events in your area. List organisations that run events, and sign up for their newsletters.

4. Ask friends and colleagues if they can share information about any networking organisations they have found valuable.

5. Note down in your calendar all the events that interest you for the next six months. Make networking an important appointment in your schedule.

6. Research professional organisations that could be relevant for your personal development, and find out if they have networking events you can attend.

7. Examine your existing connections. Write down everyone you know. If you are on Facebook, this could already be your friends list — start thinking about people they may know who you wish to know.

8. Think about your ideal client. What do they look like? Where will they go? How will you know when you have found them? Visualise meeting them and how you will connect with them.

9. Evaluate the services you need. Networking is not just about selling yourself. You may be looking for suppliers and associates. Think about what resources you might need.

10. Shift your mindset. Don't approach networking thinking "what is in it for me?" Start thinking about how you can contribute to others instead. This is the most important mindset of an effective networker.

PRE-EVENT PREPARATION

2

"I run on the road long before I dance under the lights."

Muhammad Ali

Preparing for networking is really important. Some of the items in this chapter may seem completely obvious. However, I've personally slipped up on many occasions, so I hope you can learn from my mistakes. Trust me, you can save yourself hassle and headaches if you plan ahead.

Choosing your first networking events

In the previous chapter we looked at setting objectives and pinpointing the best networking events to attend. In the mid to long term this will be essential, but in the short term start off with some 'soft landing' events. If you are new to networking, you will need to build your confidence, and some events will be better for this than others. For example, if you go to a lunchtime talk or a social event, you may find the crowd a bit cold and unreceptive to networking. A wine-tasting event may seem like a great place to network, but it may not be the best place to do so. You'll probably find that people are more likely to go to such events with small groups of friends rather than alone, so it could be difficult for you to break into groups without intruding on conversations.

If you choose an event that is specifically set up for people to network, you'll find the natives are much friendlier and open to being approached. Most Chambers of Commerce will run such events.

 Danger Zone

For your first few events, it's a good idea to avoid breakfast meetings. People are often in a hurry to get back to work so their time is limited. I also suggest you avoid events that will be serving lots of alcohol — you need to hone your skills before you can deliver them under the influence! Both of these types of events will be excellent in the future, but they are not the best to start with. Try a coffee morning or perhaps a lunch.

Enlist a wingman

Perhaps the scariest thing about a networking event is walking into a room alone. Make it easier by bringing a friend so you can arrive together and even initially stand together to assess the room and form a plan. You could then invite others to join in your conversation and begin networking.

Danger Zone

Networking with friends is easy, but you have to ensure that you don't just end up talking to your friends. Go with friends to give you courage, but you must split up and become confident enough to network on your own.

Check the venue location

Find your venue on Google maps. Be clear if you are going to an office, a restaurant or a conference centre, and print out specific instructions of exactly where you are going. On my way to an event, I once dropped my iPhone, which smashed and died. All the details of where I was going were in an email and I had not printed it out. That meant I had no idea of where I was going as all the details were on my phone.

It also helps to check where the parking is or to research your public transport routes beforehand.

Make sure you know which floor you are going to, and which entrance to use. Do you need any ID to get into the building? I've been caught out without a photo ID when one has been required. Is there a telephone number you can source before the event in case you get lost? I frequently witness people turning up late and flustered at events due to all these factors.

Danger Zone

I was so nervous about attending my first networking event that when I left the house I didn't realise there was hardly any fuel in my car, and I ran out of petrol on the way. I arrived at my first event 45 minutes late, flustered and even more embarrassed than I should have been. Don't let this happen to you. Treat a networking event like an interview. Turn up early and make an impactful first impression.

Decide on an impactful outfit

As an image consultant, I could write an entire book on this subject, but this Success Skills series already has a book called *Professional Image: Your Roadmap to Success* by Pang Li Kin, so I'll recommend you read that book and will keep this section as brief as I can.

What you choose to wear to your networking event is vitally important. Information enters our brain twice as fast through our eyes than it does through our ears, so people will register and remember what they see rather than what they heard.

1. Represent yourself and your personal brand

What you wear sends messages about your personal and business values.

If you were to place a product on a shelf you would package it to attract customers. Package yourself wisely. Ensure the outer packaging represents what is on the inside. Think about the type of connections you are looking to attract and make sure you are sending the right messages to attract these connections. (This is why we call it the business dating game!)

Let's explore the main areas that you need to consider when dressing for your event.

2. Colour

A colourful outfit will always help if you want to be remembered. Think about it. If I call you to follow up after the event and you have forgotten who I am, would it help if I say, "Remember me? I was the one wearing black trousers and a white shirt!" Yeah, right! That would be me and many others at the event. However, if I were the one wearing the red dress or the great zebra print shoes, it would be a different story.

Wearing the right colours for your complexion will make you look healthier. If you wear colourful clothes, you will also appear more confident even if you don't feel it yet. Ladies, it is very easy for you to choose a colourful dress or silk blouse when you are going to be networking. Gentlemen, in today's largely smart casual business environment your power suit will be the power shirt. Choose a striped or checked shirt in bolder colours rather than a plain dreary pastel.

I would urge you to find an image consultant and find out what colours suit you. For both women and men, this can transform your life. You will know what colour clothes to buy and how to combine them so that you make a great visual impact. For the price of a night out you can take away the guesswork.

3. Be current

This is my personal exasperation! Did you purchase your clothes this century? I constantly see people wearing tired old shirts with curly collars, and suits that are obviously over 20 years old. If you would like to convince me that you are successful, innovative, creative and a blue-sky thinker, then dress the part — invest in yourself!

If you are a knowledgeable, skilled expert in your field and selling your consulting genius for a premium price, then don't leave me wondering, "If she is so successful with all these great clients, then why can she not afford a decent haircut?" People buy from people. You are your greatest advertisement. Pay close attention to your personal packaging.

Ensure your image is congruent with your brand.

Fast Fact

Creating a professional wardrobe does not have to cost a lot. Shop in budget shops, buy second hand, swap clothes with friends. If you want to become phenomenally successful, you need to look like you already are. Find a way to invest in your image and you will reap the rewards.

Use the form below to evaluate where you might need to make some changes.

	Absolutely	Might need some work	Oops!
I wear impactful colours that will get me noticed, and I know that they suit me.			
I know which styles, cuts and fabrics flatter my bodyline and make me feel confident about my appearance.			
My clothes reflect my personality and represent the image I would like to project for myself and my organisation.			
I carry a smart sophisticated notepad, pen, phone, laptop.			
I have a great capsule work wardrobe for mix-and-match separates that I can use to create impactful outfits for every occasion.			
I completely understand what it means when the dress code states 'smart casual' or 'business casual'.			
I am perfectly groomed with regular haircuts, and I take care of my skin, nails, hands, etc.			
I always smell nice, and I use deodorant and aftershave/perfume.			

Prepare your elevator pitches

According to Wikipedia, "An *elevator pitch* (or *elevator speech* or *elevator statement*) is a short summary used to quickly and simply define a product, service or organisation and its value proposition. An elevator speech should sum up unique aspects of your service or product in a way that excites others."

Fast Fact

The idea behind your elevator pitch is that if you happen to step into an empty lift with the person you would most like to meet and you had the length of time to travel 10 floors, what might you say to leave an impact on this person?

In Chapter 3, we will look at where and how to use an elevator pitch, but before you attend any event you should definitely prepare one. In fact, I would recommend a small library of elevator pitches, each one a different length and targeted at a different audience.

Without doubt, the best elevator pitch is the one that you feel totally comfortable saying, and one that helps you engage in conversations easily. Let me share with you some ideas so that you can work out your perfect pitches.

1. Do you have a unique tag?

A dear friend and colleague would start his one-minute presentations with, "Good morning ladies and gentlemen, my name is John Cassidy and I shoot people for a living." After an appropriate pause, he would go on to explain he was a photographer. Using a clever spin on words and getting an audience to laugh will certainly make you memorable. Something like this is best used when you have to do a prepared thirty- or sixty-second introduction to a group.

2. Sell the benefit of your service first

Some job titles seem to have the power to immediately hit your snooze button. Amanda is an accountant. She often finds that as soon as she introduces herself, people tend to switch off. Now when someone asks her what she does, she replies with, "I help small business owners pay less tax." People will then normally go to on to ask her how she does that, and the conversation continues.

Whether this approach is right for you will really depend on your job. When I introduce myself to a group of women as a personal shopper, they are immediately fascinated and want to find out more. No clever or fancy lines required. If I were an accountant networking with small business owners, chances are one of them may actually be looking for an accountant, so I would just introduce myself as one.

3. State your job and move on quickly

In Chapter 1, I asked you to consider why you are networking and what your desired outcome is. Caroline is a project manager for a large international bank. She is networking to widen her social circle and gain connections that could help her further her career in other banking organisations. When she explains what she does, if another person is in her field, or working in a different area within her organisation, they will ask her more questions about her current position. Those who have no idea what a project manager does will not benefit from her elaborating more on her job. The best thing she can do is quickly move the conversation away from work to other mutually interesting subjects.

 Danger Zone

Prepare versions of your elevator pitch at 15, 30, 45 and 60 seconds. I've been to events with my perfectly prepared 60-second pitch and then been told to cut it to 45 seconds because too many people turned up. Know how to lengthen or shorten your pitch.

Nailing the petrifying one-minute pitch

Depending on the networking event, you may just be chatting with people generally, in which case you would often start a conversation by introducing yourself with your name and what you do. If you have to give a more formal introduction to a group, I often don't start with my name. Let me share with you some ideas from great 60-second pitches I've heard. They will hopefully inspire you to find something unique to help you stand out from the crowd.

1. Open with a question

I might ask, "How many of you have, or know someone who has, a wardrobe full of clothes with nothing to wear?" Many people in the audience will smile and nod. After a pause, I'll follow with, "How many of you have *two* wardrobes full of clothes and nothing to wear?" The audience will laugh again. Now I have their attention and can continue to explain what I do.

2. Open with an interesting statistic or fact

How about this for an opening line: "Did you know that the average women spends 3,276 hours of her life deciding what to wear? And alarmingly, she wears the same 20 per cent of her wardrobe 80 per cent of the time." Corporate decision-makers often like numbers and statistics. It gets your audience thinking, "Does that apply to me?" or "Who do I know in that catchment?"

3. Stimulate imagination with a prop

A fellow networker, Judith Larkin, did an amazing one-minute pitch with props. Judith runs a company that sources merchandise such as pens, mugs, post-its, etc. As she was talking, she had an assistant hold up samples of each item. Judith purposely spoke really quickly, listing the products she could provide one after another, while the assistant struggled to find and hold up mugs, umbrellas, pens, cuddly toys. It was funny and very visual. And it made her memorable!

4. Compose a song or a rap

I've seen this done well and also not quite so well! A friend and colleague Jaqui Rankin, a financial advisor, performs a brilliant and memorable ditty, "You want to be a billionaire so flipping bad, buy all the things you never had..." If you know that song, you'll understand how engaging it would be for a financial advisor to deliver her pitch like that. My friend and editor of this book, Shirley Taylor, delivers a mean rap and it's different each time. We all eagerly await the next monthly version!

Fast Fact

All these people I'm mentioning are real! They are my friends, my suppliers, my clients. Real people who I'm privileged to call friends and delighted to feature in the book. I met them all while networking.

5. Give an analogy

Serena Koh, a financial advisor, gave a brilliant one-minute pitch comparing health insurance for women to bras. "When you're young and perky you don't need much support, but as you get older and things start to head downhill, you may find you need more support." It was memorable, funny and real!

6. Secure your next liaison

Include a call to action in your pitch. Tell them what to do next: "Call me on…", "Sign up for my newsletter at…", "Follow me on Facebook".

7. Seal it with a kiss

However you decide to structure and present your pitch, end it with your name, even if you already gave it earlier. The majority of your audience will not pay much attention to the first five words of your pitch. If your content and presentation hooks them, you will need to say your name loudly and clearly again at the end of the presentation. They could be taking notes and need to be able to find you again.

Fast Fact

Some networking events give you a list of the guests. If the guest list is numbered that can be really useful. During my pitch I would say, "I'm Sharon Connolly, I'm number 23 on the list." This means anyone taking notes can easily find me on the guest list.

Try This

Crafting your pitches will take time and practice, and you will hone your pitches after each event. For now, jot down some ideas on the different ways you could introduce yourself. Which examples from those I've mentioned did you like? What do you think suits your brand and personality?

Fast Fact

The best elevator pitch will be the one you can confidently deliver!

Have an outstanding business card

Always have a plentiful supply of business cards that are easily accessible throughout any event. They are your networking currency. Leave business cards in every handbag, in pockets of all your coats and jackets, in the glove compartment of your car. NEVER be without your cards.

Danger Zone

Make sure your business cards are easy to access during an event. I quite often come unstuck when I have to scrabble around in my handbag for cards, for example if I have worn an outfit without a pocket. If you are holding a cup and a plate of food, you don't want to have to put it down in order to pass someone your business card.

If you work for a large company, you will probably have no influence over how your business cards look, so just make sure you have a plentiful supply. If you are in charge of your own branding and design, here are some things to consider when designing your own business card.

Buy the best quality card you can afford to demonstrate that you care about quality.

- Choose matt laminate rather than gloss. If someone wants to write on your card, it's tricky to write on glossy cards with most pens.

- Consider leaving some white or light space on your card, so that people can write notes on it.

- Do you need a photograph? As an image consultant and the face of my company, it is important that I have a photograph on my card. If this is relevant for you, make sure the photograph is current, professionally-taken and clear.

- Does your card say what you do? Be aware that someone may retrieve your card from the depths of their coat pockets years after they first met you. Does your card state what you do, and possibly even what is unique about the way that you do it?

I love my card, which was designed by my friend and graphic designer, Billie Sharp. Where do you think I met her? You guessed it — at a networking event!

 Danger Zone

In some cultures, it's bad manners to deface a business card by writing on it. Research this first if you are networking in an unfamiliar country!

Star Tips when preparing for your networking event

1. Dive in! Sign up for your first networking event and pencil more in your calendar.

2. Research exactly where you are going and how you will get there so you can avoid travel dilemmas.

3. Find an image consultant in your area and learn which colours suit you.

4. Evaluate your business wardrobe and ensure you are presenting yourself professionally.

5. Craft several versions of your elevator pitch for different durations and different audiences.

6. Brainstorm with some friends on how you might make your pitch more interesting and memorable.

7. Practise your pitch so that you are precise and confident.

8. Assess your business card. Does it convey quality? Do you need to have a redesign or reprint based on some of the advice in this chapter?

9. Stock up on business cards and store them in jackets, coats and bags so you are never without them.

10. Practise your best smile. If something does not go quite to plan, a beaming smile will often make it all OK.

PROSPECTING FOR GOLD

"There is no passion to be
found playing small — in
settling for a life that is
less than the one you are
capable of living."

Nelson Mandela

My friend Nicola is really scared of networking. She hates it. But she knows it's a brilliant way for her to grow her graphic design business. She also knows she's not the most confident person. Let me share with you how she gets herself to attend networking events.

She sees the event in a calendar. She signs up. She says to herself, "Just because I signed up, it doesn't mean I have to go. If I get something more interesting on that night I'll cancel, but I'll sign up first anyway."

The evening arrives and she tries desperately to think of any excuse not to go. She makes a deal with herself. "I'll just get changed and do my make-up. I don't have to go, but I'll just get ready and see how I feel." Still nervous, she carries on the conversation with herself. "I'll just go and see what it looks like from the outside. Perhaps I'll sit in the car and watch the people go in, just to see if it's busy and what sort of people are there."

When she gets there, she continues her baby steps to bravery. "I'll just go up the stairs. I don't have to stay, but I'll just go in and see what it's like." After five minutes up the stairs she goes in with her heart beating ten to the dozen, still giving herself permission to leave at any second. She then makes the final deal with herself, thinking, "I'll just introduce myself to one person." Ambushing the first stray person who walks past, she holds out her hand and says, "Hi, I'm Nicola." She once introduced herself to the waitress! Nicola has been really successful in growing her business through networking and has made valuable connections and great friends. Years on, she still has to go through these baby steps to success. You need to find yours.

 Aha! Moment

I'm not the only person who is scared of networking and meeting people. Practically everyone is scared!

Now that you've heard Nicola's story, what about you? You can do it too, but to save you from shaking hands with the waitress, let me share with you some other strategies to connect confidently with your fellow networkers.

Locate the hotspots

So you've booked the event and arrived. You've taken your name badge and walked into the room. Whether you are on your own or with your wingman, you now need to decide where to stand. Don't sit. Unless everyone is sitting, I suggest you don't sit down at a networking event, because you can't easily circulate and meet new people. Let's look at some strategies you can use to increase your chances of success.

To make it easier for you to meet people, it's important to find the hotspots. These are places where there will be a good flow of traffic. Normally these will be the bar or where the drinks are being served. If there is a food counter, this is a last option but still a good one. Get a drink and position yourself in a hotspot, and then decide on your plan of action. Let's explore a number of scenarios.

1. You are standing alone

Break into a conversation in a small group. When you know what you are looking for, this is actually the easiest option. You need to look for an 'open' conversation, not a 'closed' group. A closed group would be people who already know each other, or even sometimes those who have just met who are in the middle of a deep conversation, not a casual chat. You can tell by observing their body language and positioning.

Did you know that you are already a body language expert? You are programmed to pick up visual clues from postures, positions and gestures. You probably don't realise it, but you can instinctively decipher body language by listening to your intuition. People in a closed group will often have their feet pointing towards each other. Their bodies will be facing each other and they will be leaning in to each other. This could be a group of two or more. You can have six people in a closed group and two in an open group. Groups of three or more can often be open groups, but it's important to look at the body language rather than the numbers.

If they are leaning towards each other with feet pointed into the middle of the group then this is not an easy group to approach. Select a group where their bodies are turned slightly away from each other and their feet are turned out. Walk up confidently and say "Hi." Follow it with something like, "I'm new here and don't know anyone. Do you mind if I join you?" Perhaps just introduce yourself and shake hands. If you have chosen your event wisely, then that is what is expected of you. We'll discuss how to carry on the conversation later in the chapter, but you'll have broken the ice and you'll be in!

2. Save a 'Wallflower'

My friend and colleague Karen Leong often talks about rescuing wallflowers. The wallflower is the networker who is loitering at the edge of the room pretending to be looking at very urgent emails or messages on her phone. Watch her body language. Is she really looking at important messages, or is she pretending to look busy while she's secretly nervous and too scared to break into a conversation with someone? A wallflower is actually praying for someone to go and talk to them. Answer the wallflower's prayer. Walk up and introduce yourself, and say "Hello, I see you are on your own. Me too! Aren't these events scary when you are new?" And that's it, you're in!

3. Snag a wanderer

A wallflower pretends to be dealing with very important emails, while a wanderer strides confidently... nowhere. A wanderer may have already connected with some people and be looking for the next group to chat to. Sometimes the wanderer will be confident and experienced; sometimes he might be new like you. Wanderers are easy to connect with. Catch their eye, smile and they'll connect with you.

If you smile at a wanderer, he is very likely to stop and say, "Hi! Did we meet at an event previously?" Say "No", introduce yourself and you're in!

4. Floaters

You can save a floater, but please don't ever be one! A floater is someone who is sort of in a conversation but not quite. More frequently seen at a seated event, and often in the middle of two groups, a floater might have said one or two words to a group on one side of them, and perhaps one or two words to a group on the other side. The floater is on the outskirts, not confident enough to break in and actually join a conversation. If you are in a conversation with a floater, save them! Invite them in, move the chairs. It's a horrible position to be in!

Now that I've given you a few scenarios of how you can break into conversations, let's move on to look at what you can say.

Use your elevator pitch

In the last chapter, we discussed your elevator pitch. When someone asks what you do — and they will — you should have your chosen elevator pitch rehearsed and ready to go. If you have planned it well, that should be enough to move the conversation forward.

Aim and fire

This is my favorite technique, and much more effective if you are selling a product or service. To use this effectively, I usually start with my "What do you do?" question, then find out more about the person and try to see how I can help them. I may have a product or service that is perfect for them, or I may have a referral or connection that I can pass on. Here are three conversations that could happen.

Conversation #1

"Hi, I'm Sharon, nice to meet you."

"Hi, I'm Sarah, good to meet you too."

"What do you do, Sarah?"

"I'm an Office Manager for Tan & Wee Partnership, a firm of lawyers specialising in employment law."

"Ah really, how interesting, and do you find that you get many contacts from networking?" (it doesn't matter whether she answers yes or no)

"Do you ever run your own in-house events?"

"Yes, we do. We run quarterly events to advise our clients on new developments in the legal profession."

"That's great, and how many women do you get at those events?"

"Oh, not that many at all. You know, we have a lot of female clients but we just don't get them to come along to that type of event."

"Ah, let me share something with you. I've partnered with a lot of law firms in the past, helping them to run networking events. It's amazing. If you invite your female clients along to an evening to learn about the latest tax incentives, no one attends. But invite them to an evening with a speaker on how to look younger and slimmer, and you'll have standing room only."

"Oh, that's interesting."

"Absolutely. I work with lots of speakers who might be able to come along and help you build better relationships with your clients. Whatever you are looking for, I should be able to connect you."

Fast Fact

It's not always about you selling your product. If your conversation uncovers a problem that you cannot provide a solution for, but you know someone who can provide that solution, then share that information. Networking is about giving and sharing!

Conversation #2

"Hi, I'm Sharon Connolly. Nice to meet you."

"Hi, Bradley Thomas from Hewlett Packard."

"Oh HP, fantastic. What do you do there?"

"Well, I'm a sales manager. I take care of small office equipment for all of Asia Pacific.

"Wow, impressive. So do you have a team of salespeople working for you?"

"Yes, actually I have a team of 25 salespeople, some based here and others based throughout the region."

"Oh, I see. It must be challenging to manage all of them! I'm sure it keeps you on your toes!"

"Haha, yes it does. Tell me Sharon, what do you do?"

(At this stage I know that he has a team of salespeople! I run training for salespeople! So now I'll go back with my pitch.)

"Well, you know your team of salespeople. Have any of them ever turned up for work dressed inappropriately? Do you ever look at them and think, 'Did you get dressed in the dark?'"

"Oh yes, all the time. It's a big problem and I don't know how to solve it."

"Well, part of my job that I enjoy most is running training courses for teams like yours to ensure that their image doesn't let their organisation down!"

And now we're off and running! I would then dig around and find out how I might be able to help him in delivering a solution.

Danger Zone

In these two examples, I do come a little close to selling. I wouldn't advise you to sell at networking events. They are all about building relationships, not selling. But in these two examples, I've given my contact a hook of how what I do might be of interest to them. I'll leave it there and move on to get to know the person better. I don't want to sell without first developing the relationship.

Conversation #3

"Good morning, I'm Sharon Connolly. Pleased to meet you."

"Morning, George Grant from APB Plumbing Services."

"Ah excellent, George. We all need a plumber at one time or another. May I take a couple of cards from you so that I have one on hand, or can pass it on to anyone looking for a plumber?"

As an image consultant, I'm unlikely to have much business synergy with a plumber, so I've acknowledged his profession and offered to help him in the future. As he takes his cards out of his wallet, I notice pictures of his wife and children.

"Ah, what beautiful children. How old are they?"

"Gemma is two and Charlie is four. That's my wife, Anna."

"Oh they are delightful. You must be very proud. Is Anna a full-time mum?"

"Yes she is, she does a little bit of admin work for me, but she looks after those little monsters."

"Wow, that's a full-time job in itself. My children are much older now but I remember what it was like to be on the go chasing a two- and a four-year-old around all day."

After a brief pause, George should now think about turning the conversation back to me.

"So what do you do, Sharon?"

"Well, I'm an image consultant, and I actually often work with busy mums like Anna to help them find time to understand what to wear and how to look their best. I show them how to dress like a 'yummy mummy'. It's an amazing job, so much fun, and I know I make a huge difference to my clients. When you are looking for a special present for Anna sometime, it might just make you husband of the year."

I then pass him my business card.

Danger Zone

Remember in the last chapter I urged you to have your business cards easily accessible? If someone asks you for a card, you don't want to be scrabbling around in your bag or pockets looking for one. Make sure they are always close at hand.

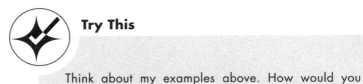

Try This

Think about my examples above. How would you have moulded your product or service in the examples given? Practise thinking on your feet!

How would you have connected to:

a) George, the plumber?

_____

_____

b) Sarah, the Office Manager in the law firm?

_____

_____

c) Bradley, the Sales Manager from HP?

_____

_____

My 'aim and fire' technique requires you to be a really fast thinker and know how your business proposition can be the solution for many problems. If George the plumber had been divorced, I would know that he possibly had trouble shopping for himself if his ex-wife used to do the shopping. If Anna had been working full time then I'd know she'd have no time to shop and might need a personal shopper. This technique is about thinking on your feet. Ask questions to find a problem, and then think about how you might provide a solution.

How's your handshake and posture?

Have you ever had feedback on your handshake? Have you ever thought about it?

It is said that the handshake was originally a gesture where counterparts would grab the wrist of the person approaching them to check for concealed weapons when first meeting. Rumoured to have been introduced to western culture by Sir Walter Raleigh, a handshake is now the normal etiquette for meeting and greeting around the world.

Let's take a look at what makes a good handshake:

- Ensure that your palms are not clammy and sweaty. If this is a problem for you, spray your hands with anti-perspirant before networking. No one wants to feel a damp handshake, and wiping your hands on your trousers before offering your hand will not win you any etiquette prizes.

- If you have come in from the cold, rub your hands together first so they are warmer. A freezing cold handshake is not good.

- Confidently offer your hand to the other person, leaning forward and bending your elbow at 90 degrees.

- Match up the palms of your hands as best as you can, and grip with the thumbs.

- A firm grasp is best in most Western cultures.

- Smile and maintain eye contact as you introduce yourself with enthusiasm.

- Shake two to three times.

- Release your grip and move back, continuing with the smile and eye contact.

Danger Zone

If you are working internationally, it is really important to find out what the normal greeting is in other cultures. In Japan and China, a weak, limp handshake is preferred. In Muslim countries, women often prefer not to shake hands or make eye contact. Check that you know what is appropriate if you are visiting another country.

Your posture is also important at networking events. Stand tall and proud. If you are not feeling confident, then ensure that you at least look confident. Stand with your feet about hip distance apart. Keep your shoulders back and hold your head up high. You might feel like a frightened mouse on the inside but don't let it show!

Start imagining yourself as confident, courageous and charming, and you soon will be.

Visualisation

Visualisation is a powerful tool often used by athletes to gain a competitive advantage. I use it all the time when I'm nervous about a presentation that I am giving. Before the event, I visualise what will happen at the end of the event: usually after I finish my talk, the audience will clap. I may even get a standing ovation. As I step down from the stage, delegates will approach me to tell me how much they've enjoyed my talk and how they would love to have me come and talk to their company. Others will come up to me and tell me which parts of my talk really resonated with them. I visualise emails in my inbox the following morning thanking me for the inspiration. I visualise what will happen, and it often comes true. I have a song on my iPod that I listen to when I do this visualisation, and if I ever feel nervous I just listen to the song and instantly have images of a successful outcome. This always outweighs any nerves and anxiety. Why don't you try it?

 Try This

Now, and before your networking event, close your eyes and imagine yourself striding confidently into the event venue. See yourself shaking hands and smiling confidently, chatting away with many fellow networkers and new friends. Visualise exchanging business cards, and people listening attentively as you talk. Can you see it? Keep visualising until the images are so clear in your head that you feel like you are watching a movie.

In this chapter I have given you some ideas on how you might more confidently overcome your nerves and break into conversations. In subsequent chapters we'll look how to continue the conversations and move around, but for now you're 'in' and you're chatting. That's a brilliant start. Still feeling nervous? Remember Nicola and her baby steps at the beginning of the chapter — one small step at a time!

Star Tips when prospecting for gold

1. Locate the networking hotspots as soon as you arrive at an event; these are the places where you will encounter the most traffic.

2. Survey the room and learn to recognise open and closed groups from the position of their feet and bodies.

3. Improve your posture. Stand up straight and tall so you look confident.

4. Review your handshake. Get feedback from friends on how you meet and greet.

5. Scan the room for wallflowers, wanderers and floaters. These people will love you for talking to them.

6. Every time you meet someone, think about how you or the people in your network could provide solutions to their problems.

7. Use positive visualisation by creating your own networking success 'movie'. Replay it often to become more confident.

8. Brainstorm the problems that you can help people to solve. Think about all the different types of people that you might meet, the problems they may have, and how you could adapt your service offerings to solve their problems.

9. Pay more attention to what your close friends and colleagues do. Remember that you may solve problems by recommending someone else's services. Start a mental or actual database of what other people in your network do.

10. Practise your widest most genuine smile. It truly is an asset in networking

BUILDING RAPPORT WITH ANYONE AND EVERYONE

*"Do not forget small kindnesses
and do not remember small faults."*

Chinese Proverb

4

In the last chapter, we looked at breaking the ice and starting conversations. Now we must go deeper and learn how to continue your conversations so that you build relationships with your networking contacts. To be truly successful at networking, you need to work hard to build meaningful relationships and nurture those relationships. In this chapter, I will help you to do that, starting with some easy tips to build rapport.

Rapport comes from the French verb '*rapporter*' which means 'to carry something back'. This is what we should aim to do when building rapport with another person — find common ground and things to agree on so you can move the conversation forward. Think of it like a game of catch — you need to pass the ball backwards and forwards without dropping it. The equivalent to dropping the ball in a conversation is standing there with nothing to say to each other!

I'm going to share with you some great ways to help build rapport with someone you have just met. If you follow these tips, everyone you meet will think you are the most charming person they have ever met.

Schmooze with small talk

What do you talk about once you have finished the initial pleasantries and introductions? You move to small talk. Small talk is generally the term used for an appropriate conversation with a stranger. The most common topic for small talk would probably be the weather, but there are lots of other small talk subjects that are equally as effective.

What you must look for is a topic that you can agree on. If it's raining outside you could start a conversation with "Wow, the rain outside is dreadful today, isn't it?" The other person is highly unlikely to respond with "No, I love the rain!" The weather is a great small talk topic as most people can agree on what is good and what is bad weather. The subject matter is not so important; it's moving the conversation forward in agreement.

Another example could be the journey to the networking event. Discuss how you got there, whether the roads were congested, if the public transport was busy, clean and on time. Try to find a topic of conversation that you can agree on so you can make a connection. Then you can start to find out a little more about each other, looking for common ground.

It's rare that we don't agree about the weather!

If your networking goals are to win business or find suppliers, you could steer the conversation back towards business, but try to find out more about the people that you are networking with rather than just what they do at work.

Try This

Make a list of subjects that you could talk about, which most people would agree with.

_____

_____

_____

_____

Activate your listening skills

If you want someone to think you are interesting, then you just have to listen to them. For many of us, it's a sad fact that we are not often listened to. Our spouse doesn't listen to us, our children don't listen, perhaps our boss never seems to hear what we are saying. So if someone takes the time to listen to what you are saying at a networking event, it can make you feel very special.

Fast Fact

There is more to listening than simply letting the words drift in through your ears.

Active listening

Active listening is a skill you need to practise. After a short while it will become second nature and you'll find it easy, but to begin with you'll need to concentrate and practise. It can make a huge difference to the person who is talking. When you are listening to someone, try some of these techniques so they know you are listening:

Non-verbal active listening

- Nod your head in agreement with what the speaker is saying.

- Show concern on your face when they are talking about a bad experience or something unpleasant.

- Activate your eyebrows. Raise them when something is surprising or very interesting to you.

- Tilt your head to one side and lean slightly forward towards the person to indicate you are really interested in what they are saying.

Verbal active listening

- Add statements such as "I see", "Really", "Interesting", "I hear what you're saying", "I feel that way too", or just "Mmm", "Uh-huh" to show that you are hearing what they are saying.

- Using repetition can be really powerful. Simply repeat the last thing that they said to you. For example, they say "I recently worked on a charity project building houses in Cambodia." You say "Houses in Cambodia, wow! Tell me more."

Danger Zone

These are all brilliant tools to help you become and active listener. However, don't overuse any of them, or you may come over as false and insincere.

The importance of body language

A substantial part of the way we communicate with each other is non-verbal. We are all already experts at expressing our feelings through our body language and reading the signals that others send out. We are naturally programmed with these skills, and body language can be understood by all cultures. If someone shakes their fist angrily at you, you'll understand them whatever language they speak!

Much of our body language is involuntary, but when communicating with others and wanting to make an impact, you must be aware of the unconscious messages you may be sending to make sure they are congruent with your intentions. For example, if you are practising active listening but gazing out of the window then your co-networker will know that you are not interested in them. So what can you do to ensure your body language supports your intentions to be a great networker?

1. Mirroring

Using subtle mirroring is a great way to build rapport. I emphasise subtle here because, as with active listening, if you overdo mirroring it will be very obvious. To mirror someone, you adopt similar body language and positioning to theirs. If they step closer towards you to speak more intently, then you take a tiny step forward too. If they pause and pick up their drink or plate of food, then you do the same. Mirroring is very evident in couples who are romantically involved. Next time you are in a restaurant, take a few minutes to look around and study couples. You'll be able to spot the lovers because, without even knowing it, they will be mirroring each other a lot.

How can you adopt this in networking? If you are sitting, you can cross your legs when your partner does. If you are standing, consider crossing your arms if your partner crosses hers. Mirroring can be really effective, but be subtle or you'll be caught out.

2. Minimising the difference

This is a slightly safer alternative to mirroring, although it works along the same lines. Rather than actually copying your partner, just ensure that you are not too different. Firstly, are you on the same level as they are? It's difficult to hold a meaningful conversation when you are sitting down and your partner is standing. If you are sitting down when someone comes to talk to you, either offer him a chair next to you or stand up and be at the same level.

Most importantly, minimise the difference between mood and enthusiasm. I'm loud, enthusiastic and motivated, so I normally spring into a networking event like Tigger. If my partner is quiet and shy, I need to speak in a softer voice and tone down my enthusiasm so she doesn't feel intimidated. I would hope that some of my enthusiasm might be infectious and that she might start to feel more confident and energised, and raise her energy to match mine.

If your partner is telling you about something serious, don't start cracking jokes. If he seems to want the conversation to be strictly business, then don't start asking him about his favourite place to holiday.

I find minimising the difference fascinating when it comes to accents. I grew up in Berkshire in England, where the Queen lives, the home of Windsor Castle and Eton College. This is possibly the world's best place to develop a well-spoken English accent. As a professional speaker and trainer, I work hard to use my Berkshire accent to speak clearly and concisely to a global audience. However, my family comes from the East End of London. If I start speaking to a Londoner, you'll quickly hear my Berkshire accent slip as I start to sound like a cockney. I lived in Australia for a year, so when speaking to Australians I'll use some of my old Aussie phrases. When speaking to an American, I will substitute American words for British ones. For example, instead of saying emptying the bin I will use taking out the trash! A lot of this is subconscious, but my brain knows that if I minimise the difference between myself and my partner, then I will build rapport more easily.

Here are some more ideas about how you can minimise the difference:

- Volume of speech. You can speak more loudly or softly.

- Speed of conversation. Opt to speak faster or slower.

- Enthusiasm. You could be more or less animated.

- Accent, if applicable.

- Vocabulary. If your partner uses long descriptive words then you could flower up your vocabulary a bit too.

- Posture. If your partner is standing very tall with great posture, make sure you're not slumping!

Fast Fact

By practising the tips in this book you are taking the initiative to make every networking connection a successful one. Your partner may or may not be an expert networker. They may not show you that they are a great listener or mirror your body language. If they do, then that's great. Both of you will build rapport and connect quickly. But if your partner does not have great networking skills, then by using yours, networking will more pleasurable for them too.

Becoming an expert connector

When you use active listening, you can make your partner feel like the most important person in the room. Even if you and your partner have no networking goals in common, even if you could never do business together or become friends, there will always be an opportunity for you to become a powerful connector. Expert networkers are expert connectors.

Fast Fact

Even if you have nothing in common with your partner, you can help them and yourself by listening carefully to their needs and thinking of possible connections in your network.

If you are struggling to find a way to build rapport with your partner, or perhaps you are getting along famously but you just cannot see any synergy between your networking goals, then ask the question: "Who are you looking to connect with at this networking event?" Perhaps drill a little deeper by asking, "What would be the ideal opportunity for you at this time?" Once you have a clear idea of how you can help someone, you are in the most powerful networking position there is. After they have shared their goals with you, you may immediately realise you have contacts within your networking circle, friends and family that might be of interest to them. If not, then you need to mentally store the information about their ideal connection and opportunity in case you can help them later.

Fast Fact

Successful networkers are selfless. They do everything they can to help others become successful. They believe it is not about them; it is what they can do for others. Call it the power of the universe, synchronicity or luck, but the most successful networkers go out of their way to help others. I can recommend a delightful book called the *The Go-Giver: A Little Story About a Powerful Business Idea* by Bob Burg and John David Mann, in which you can read more about this concept.

Exiting the conversation

So far we have been looking at breaking into conversations and moving the conversation forward, but what happens when you have exhausted the conversation or just want to move on? It depends on the goals that you set for yourself in Chapter 1, but I would recommend that you aim to come away from each networking event with five great connections. Not 25 randomly collected business cards, but five great contacts that are good connections for you or for others in your network. In order to do this, you have to be able to exit a conversation and move on to the next one. Also, if you have been unable to build rapport or your partner is practically pinning you to the wall trying to sell you something, you will want to make a quick exit. In situations like this, you could:

- Say you need to get a drink.

- Say you need to get food.

- Excuse yourself to go to the bathroom.

- Say there is someone else that you have just seen across the room.

These are some standard exit tactics, but as an expert networker you can do better. Firstly, if it is a networking event then it is completely acceptable to say, "Lovely to have met you. I'll be in touch shortly but as it's a networking event let's both circulate and meet some more people. That's what we're here for!" Don't just excuse yourself from your partner. Encourage them to go out and network effectively too.

Earlier in this chapter, we discussed being a great connector. This is also a brilliant way to exit from a conversation. You have found out who your partner is dying to meet at this event. You have found out their ideal business opportunity. Exit the conversation by offering to help them. For example you could say, "Well Bob, I understand you are looking for anyone with a small business who might be interested in renting some office space in your serviced offices. I'm going to go off and network with the rest of the room now, but if I find anyone who might be interested in some office space I'll bring them over and introduce them to you. Would that be okay?" You've just offered to be an unpaid sales representative for Bob. See how quickly he will be happy for you to move on so that you can spread the word about him. It's an easy exit strategy and a win-win situation.

Assuming Bob is a nice genuine guy, do what you have promised. Look out for opportunities for him and graciously introduce him to anyone who may be interested in his services. Do this a few times and you will quickly be the hottest networking contact at every event!

Trawling for your big fish

In his book *The Jelly Effect*, Andy Bounds gives brilliant advice on how to really work the room with charm and panache. I love the way he talks about trying to catch your big fish — the person that you really want to meet at a networking event. They are the ones who will either help you directly with your networking goals, or be able to put you in front of your major stakeholders. I aim to come away from every networking event with the business cards of at least five big fish.

Trying to catch your big fish at a networking event is just like being out on a lake fishing. You'll cast your net and occasionally reel in an old boot. An old boot is normally someone who is out for themselves, someone who often starts their conversations with a hard sell or will just bore the pants off you! When you realise that you are talking to an old boot, you will need to exit the conversation as quickly as possible. Use one of the strategies that I mentioned earlier and move on.

As well as old boots, you'll also come across tiddlers. Tiddlers are little fish, and you'll find whole shoals of them swimming at networking events. Tiddlers may be of interest to you in the future, but right now, they are not your big fish, so don't spend too much time with them. Get their business card, connect with them after the event and stay in touch; but currently they are not where you should be focusing your networking efforts. It's big fish you need to look for.

When you meet a big fish and start a great conversation, it can be tempting to stick with them for the duration of the event. You won't be able to believe your luck, knowing you've met exactly the person you were hoping to meet. Your conversation is flowing, you are building rapport... and now you need to move on! Yes, it's true! Your goal is to meet as many big fish as possible at this event, and you may not be a big fish for this person, so don't monopolise their time. When you have met your big fish and established great rapport, arrange to meet them for coffee to continue the conversation. Take your diary, and make an appointment there and then for a subsequent meeting. Thank your contact and move on to find the next one. How amazing would it be to leave every event with five appointments and brilliant new connections? Wouldn't that be better than leaving with one appointment or even none?

 Aha! Moment

The real networking takes place after the event. The networking event is just to skim through the contacts and find the ones that I really want to connect with.

 Try This

Research a number of great venues for those follow-up coffee meetings, somewhere quiet with great service. Then you'll be able to suggest something straight away when someone agrees to meet you for coffee. Go there often and get to know the staff, so they will give you better service. This will add to your credibility.

Star Tips for building rapport with anyone and everyone

1. Practise active listening techniques. It will really make the person who is talking to you feel valued.

2. Listen more than you talk. You have two ears and one mouth, so use them in that ratio.

3. Practise your small talk wherever you can — standing in the queue to get your coffee, waiting for a lift, wherever you can strike up a short conversation with strangers to build your confidence and practise your charm.

4. Become aware of your own body language. Stand in front of the mirror and watch your unconscious habits. Fix any annoying habits or incongruent faux pas.

5. Become more aware of your voice. Record yourself and study your voice. Speed up, slow down, raise and lower your tone so that you can more easily use your voice as a tool to build rapport.

6. Record networking objectives of every contact that you meet. Listen out for opportunities that you can pass on to your network.

7. Practise exiting conversations gracefully. Rather than heading off in search of the bar or the washroom, learn gracious exit strategies.

8. Go to events with a clear picture of who your big fish is, and recognise whether each contact you meet is a big fish, a tiddler or an old boot.

9. Quickly and politely move on from tiddlers and old boots to maximise your networking time.

10. Arrange to have coffee with your big fish at a later date and continue to fish for more contacts.

MAKING YOURSELF MEMORABLE

5

"Excuse me, could you step aside. You are standing in my spotlight."

Lady Gaga

After overcoming your nerves and actually getting yourself out there, one of your next biggest challenges is being memorable. When you have practised all the tips I've given you so far, you'll become an expert at finding events and working the room, but it is very important that you make yourself memorable. Building a successful network is like recruiting a whole army of employees who then go and spread your message on your behalf. Whether you are looking for a new job, new clients or new suppliers, by building a strong network you can have hundreds of people passing on your details and looking for opportunities for you every day — but in order for them to be your walking ambassadors they must remember you. In this chapter, we'll look at how you can make yourself memorable.

Presence

Some people are lucky enough to just have presence. You can't quite put your finger on it but when they walk into a room, people notice. These people seem to have an aura that lights up a room and lifts any conversation. You immediately warm to them and want to see and hear more. Certain people just seem to be born with this amazing natural charismatic magnetism! If you are not one of these lucky people, then you are going to have to study the attributes of those with presence and try to emulate them.

Your challenge in networking is to very quickly become unforgettable for the right reasons, to make a great first impression and leave a lasting one. To do this, you need to pay special attention to how you dress, your body language, your spoken voice, and let's not forget your manners.

Looking the part

I belong to a group called Asia Professional Speakers Singapore. We have monthly meetings and always make time for networking. At a recent meeting I introduced myself to a first-time visitor (let's call her Mary). She told me we had met before, twice. She said that following our first meeting she'd looked at my website and watched some of my YouTube videos, which she had enjoyed. Mary told me about herself and what she did. I felt terrible, as I had absolutely no recollection of meeting this lady before. At the end of our conversation she told me that I was not the first person at this event who had not remembered her, and she asked for my advice on being more memorable.

Mary was wearing a grey dress. It was a really nice dress but it was grey and plain, so she just blended in and looked, well, grey. I suggested that she should try wearing a brighter colour. The next time I saw her she had a fantastic cerise pink dress on. The following month at the meeting, when she was wearing a great red blouse, she shared with me that wearing the pink dress had made a huge difference. She said now when she attends networking events she's recognised and remembered.

I touched on image in Chapter 2, and I now want to talk about dressing for success in more detail. This is important. First impressions really do count, and it is vital that you make an impactful first impression and leave a lasting one. It's also important that you are consistent and pay close attention to your image. Here are some important considerations.

Quality

Why are some people so obsessed with cheap? Why do so many people want to buy cheap clothes? Don't you deserve the best? I urge you to invest in yourself and your wardrobe and value yourself. Do you want a highly paid job or a client that pays you handsomely for a job well done? If so, you must make sure you look the part.

Cheap clothes look cheap. Now I love a bargain as much as the next person but I do not wear cheap clothes. I invest in the best quality that I can afford, and so should you. Take care in your choice of fabrics. Opt for natural fabrics rather than synthetics, and pay attention to detail and quality. If you can't afford great quality new clothes, consider buying them second-hand. I gat a lot of my clothes from ebay.com.

Do a wardrobe audit and take a close look at your clothes. If you would not wear it to the most important interview of your life then it should not be hanging in your wardrobe. Every day of your life is an important interview when you grow your business by networking.

Discard your old, tired clothes and ensure that you are dressing for success. Have a look in your wardrobe and check items for these things:

- Buttons should be sewn on securely with no hanging threads

- Zippers should lay flat

- Hemming should not visible

- Trousers should be hemmed to the correct length, not dragging on the floor

- Jacket sleeves should be the right length, the edge of the jacket resting at the top of the thumb, unless they are bracelet length for ladies

- Discard any fabrics that have turned shiny from excess pressing

- Worn collars and cuffs on shirts

- Bobbling and pilling on knitwear and synthetics

- Stains and marks that you cannot get rid of

Throw out any black clothes that have faded to grey or are showing white around the seams. Get yourself some large bags and sort your clothes into things you need to throw out and those that need attention, such as mending or cleaning, and make it a priority to action this.

If your wardrobe is lacking quality clothing then you need to make an investment in buying some new clothes. You don't need to buy designer but you do need to buy quality pieces that are current. It's vital that your look reflects your personal brand and conveys the message that you want to put across.

I recently worked with Alex, who wanted to grow his new graphics design company through networking. At his first event he turned up in a very nice navy suit with a lovely red tie. Alex looked amazing — or at least he would have if he were a banker. Alex was looking for clients who wanted him to be creative, cool and funky. After working with me, Alex turned up at networking events in jeans, funky trainers and a leather jacket. Still smart, immaculately groomed and well presented, but he now looked in keeping with his brand, and prospective clients trusted that he would be a creative input to their graphics work.

Fast Fact

Dressing to reflect the brand that you are trying to portray puts trust in your prospective clients.

Colour

Colour can really help you to be memorable. Wearing black trousers and a white shirt will have you being mistaken for the serving staff. It's vital that you put a spark of colour into your networking wardrobe. As I mentioned earlier, it is a wise investment to visit an image consultant and find out which colours suit your complexion and also consider the psychological effects of colour. Just as companies invest millions into researching which colours convey the right message for their logos and packaging, you too should consider the psychological effect of your personal packaging.

Colour	Positive Attributes	Negative Attributes	Illustration: When to wear	Illustration: When NOT to wear
Red	Confident, Extroverted, Risk-taking, Leadership, Passionate, Exciting, Dramatic	Aggressive, Domineering, Attention-seeking, Dangerous	Wear when you want to be recognised and stand out in a group. Prepare to back this up with your behaviour!	At an interview. You'll potentially come across as a domineering power-seeker.
Black	Sophisticated, Mysterious, Elegant, Classy, Dramatic	Unoriginal, Uncreative, Depressing, Mournful, Heavy, Indecisive	At a formal dinner party if you do not want to overly stand out.	If you want to appear accessible to people and want them to be open with you. Black is one of the most distance-inducing shades.
White	Orderly, Innocent, Fresh, Peaceful, Clean	Over-fussy, Non-communicating, Sterile, Cold	If you need to project maximum standards of hygiene and care.	If you do not take the time for faultless grooming, as white shows every mark and stain easily.
Grey	Balanced, Modest, Reliable	Uncreative, Boring, Conservative, Unwilling to commit	At a negotiation meeting, or at interview (unless being interviewed for a creative position).	In a creative position, or working with children (grey can make children feel anxious).

Colour	Positive Attributes	Negative Attributes	Illustration: When to wear	Illustration: When NOT to wear
Navy	Dignified, Wealthy, Logical, Organised, Knowledge, Powerful, Trustworthy	Conservative, Dull, Not innovative	When you need to look authoritative and in charge.	If you want to stand out at a business conference.
Brown	Solid, Earthy, Natural, Approachable, Mothering, Robust	Unsophisticated, Conservative, Common, Safe, Boring	Brown is the least threatening colour to others, so wear it when you want people to open up to you.	If you need to be assertive and powerful in a business situation.
Green	Tranquil, Balanced, Fresh, Helpful, Informal, Nurturing	Predictable, Unmotivated, Shy, Jealous	Wear green when feeling particularly tired or tense. It induces a sense of calm.	If you're an entrepreneur. Green will not inspire confidence in your drive and motivation.
Yellow	Youthful, Happy, Outgoing, Creative, Experimental, Fun	Impulsive, Disorganised, Juvenile, Cowardly, Volatile, Frivolous	When working with children. It's the number one colour children respond to the most, and is the most visible colour to the human eye.	In business situations. A subtle yellow accent, such as a tie or stripe in a shirt is more appropriate.

Colour	Positive Attributes	Negative Attributes	Illustration: When to wear	Illustration: When NOT to wear
Blue	Calm, Friendly, Authoritative, Traditional, Inoffensive, Trustworthy	Uncreative, Depressing, Unoriginal, Dull	When being interviewed for a financial position in a traditional industry.	When you want to impress with your confidence and success.
Pink	Feminine, Approachable, Gentle	Submissive, Under-confident, Pathetic	To soften a deep coloured, masculine cut suit. Wear as an accent only. A man who wears pink exudes confidence and is comfortable with his masculinity.	Women should choose whole outfits in pink with care. Accenting is better so as not to project a "Barbie Doll" image.
Orange	Hospitable, Youthful, Sociable, Fun, Energetic	Childlike, Not very disciplined, Erratic, Common, Superficial	If you want to wear an energising colour. Do only include it as an accent.	For any business event. Orange is the least professional colour you could wear. It will immediately downgrade your status.
Purple	Sophisticated, Dramatic, Intriguing, Creative, Sensitive, Spiritual, Good listener	Day-dreaming, Weird, Impractical, Immature, Suspicious	If you are an artist of any kind, or want to project the creative side to your character.	When you wish to project balance and stability. Purple promotes the exact opposite.

Style personality

As an image consultant, I work closely with my clients to help them craft a unique style personality. Imagine that you left a suitcase of your clothes in the middle of your office. If someone opened it, would they be able to identify those clothes as yours? If the case was full of black trousers and white shirts, then it's unlikely. Where's the personality?

When I walk around in shops I can usually pick out items that would be perfect for my clients. When I send them a picture, 90 per cent of the time they love the item. I know what they like because we have worked hard to narrow down their own unique look and way of blending outfits and accessories together. Do you have your own unique look? If not, think about developing one.

But what if you are not able to use your clothes to help you stand out, perhaps because you wear a uniform, or you really don't feel comfortable expressing yourself through your clothing? In this case, you will have to work harder in other areas such as body language, communication or following up.

 Danger Zone

It is really important that your look reflects current trends. I'm not saying that you need to look like you have just walked off of the catwalk in Milan, but it is very important that your look is up to date. By 2014, 50 per cent of the workforce will be Generation Y. You will be competing against Gen Y for jobs and contracts. Gen Y will be the decision makers and the budget holders. If you are not part of this generation then you may think that fashion is not important to you, but it is important to Gen Y — they know whether your shoes are 'so last year'. To work with Gen Y, you need to gain their trust, make them feel like you understand where they are coming from. Adopting some current trends can help you do this.

Try This

Go and buy a stack of magazines. Some fashion-related, some lifestyle. Go through them and cut out pictures of clothes, looks and outfits that inspire you. Create a mood board of things you like. Choose colours and textures, even landscapes and furniture. Think about what you really like and how it inspires and relates to you. Then take a look in your wardrobe and see if the way you choose to package yourself corresponds to what inspires you.

For some people there may be a conflict of appropriateness. If you are inspired by the Sahara Desert and yearn for floaty chiffon in rich opulent shades adorned with tassles and coins, you may have trouble bringing that into your workplace as an aspiring banker, but accents in your jewellery or the colour choices of your ties could show your personality a little more. This chapter is about being memorable, so if everyone is wearing conservative corporate clothes, your tie, necklace and shoes could be your calling card, the thing that people remember you for.

Think of each item of advice in this book like a leg on a table. I want to give you so much advice that your table has so many legs, so if you turned it upside down it would look like a hairbrush. If someone knocks away one of the legs of your table it will still stand — but if your table only had four legs, when someone knocks one away your table is very wobbly and can't stand any more.

Posture and body language

Do people look up when you walk into a room? Your posture plays a large part in your gravitas. Think about how you walk. Do you stride confidently or shuffle and slouch? Here are some tips to improve your posture:

- Put your shoulders back and down

- Pull in your abdominals

- Take deep breaths to expand your chest

- Stand tall

- Take larger steps

- Stride confidently

When you are standing and talking you should also be aware of your posture and your body language. The first step to improve your body language is to start being aware of it, and also to start consciously noticing the body language signals that others display.

Here are my top tips for demonstrating more gravitas with powerful body language:

1. Stand with your legs about hip-distance apart. It will make you appear grounded and stable.

2. Don't cross your arms. You may be perceived as being closed and uninterested.

3. Nod when you are listening to show you are interested. Practise your active listening.

4. Lean slightly towards the person you are talking to. Not too much, but just gently angle your body towards them. Be careful not to invade

their personal space. Everyone has their own comfort zones and it varies in different cultures. If someone steps back from you then you may be invading their personal space a bit too much.

5.   Avoid touching your face. Covering your mouth with your hand or touching your nose indicates that you are nervous or not being truthful. Notice if this is a habit of yours and fix it immediately.

6.   Ladies, don't twiddle your hair. It's a flirty gesture, so save it for the cocktail bar, not the networking event.

We unconsciously read body language but it doesn't always give us accurate information. Crossed arms could mean they're just cold.

7. Stop fidgeting. When someone is nervous they may shift the weight from foot to foot, fiddle with pens or wring their hands. It is very annoying if this happens when you are trying to talk to someone. Make sure you are not doing it.

8. Lower your drink or put it down. If you hold your cup of coffee at chest area, it can make you seem guarded and distant.

9. Use your hands to gesticulate. Don't go over the top, but if you speak with your hands you will seem more passionate about your subject.

10. Smile and laugh. If someone says something funny, then laugh at it! It's much easier to build relationships over more fun subjects. Try not to laugh first at your own jokes though.

11. Subtly mirror the actions of others to build rapport. If she leans forward, you might lean forward a little too. If she holds her hands on her hips, you might do the same. But don't copy others straightaway or it will look strange and you will be caught out.

12. Believe that you are confident, successful and that everyone you are talking to is interested and charmed by you. Act like you already are a successful and interesting networker. Fake it until you make it!

It will seem very strange but you have to practise these tips in front of the mirror. Top models practice for hours to ensure that they know what photography angles best suit their face and bodies. We are all different, so make sure you know what posture and body language traits work for you. Have yourself videoed while presenting. It will reveal your body language blunders and you can then take steps to fix them.

If you try adopting one or two of these body language tips every day, they will soon become second nature.

Voice

Is the way you speak an asset or a liability? Many people believe they cannot change their voice, but there is a lot you can do to improve the tone, pitch and quality of every word you speak. Record yourself having a conversation with someone. Leave it for 24 hours and then play it back. Waiting 24 hours will help detach you from the content and focus on the delivery. Listen to your voice. It will sound strange to you, because we hear our own voices differently to how others hear us, but listen to it objectively. Are there any words that you overuse? I've had a habit before of finishing a lot of sentences with "OK?" Others say words like "actually" over and over. Do you "umm" or "ah" a lot? As soon as you are made aware of something, you must take steps to correct it.

If an actor can completely change their accent for a film roll, then you can most definitely work on a few adjustments to ensure that you don't let yourself down when speaking.

Here are my top tips to seduce your audience with your velvet-toned voice:

1. Slow down! Most of us talk too fast. Simply slowing down and being a little more deliberate with our words will make it easier for others to follow us.

2. Lower the pitch of your voice. Particularly for women, if your voice is too high it can sound a little squeaky. Practise speaking at a slightly lower octave and you will sound more powerful.

3. Pause more. Every time you pause it gives your listeners another few seconds to digest what you are saying. Try lengthening the pauses you take between sentences. It also gives your brain a little more time to process what comes out of your mouth.

4. Love your accent. You don't need to lose your accent. It's part of your charm and personality. But you do need to make sure you can still pronounce words clearly so that they are understood. Check

out the website of one of the other authors in this Success Skills series, Heather Hansen. At www.englishpronunciationcourse.com, she provides help to make sure you can be clearly understood.

5. Articulate using all the muscles in your tongue, and all the muscles controlling your lips to shape the sounds. Make sure you don't slur your words together. Practise speaking in front of a mirror and record yourself.

6. Sing. Yes, sing! Depending on your voice, you may want to keep this to the privacy of the shower, the car or in a wide open space, but singing out loud is a really good exercise to help improve your voice.

Sing whenever you can. It will raise your spirits and help exercise your voice.

7. Read stories aloud to children. Really emphasise the words and get very animated with your voice. Your young audience will be enthralled, and this can help your voice become more varied and ensure that you sound passionate about your subject.

8. Practise diaphragmatic breathing. Place your hand on your stomach and take a deep breath. Inhale and breathe deeply so that you feel the breath come right down to your diaphragm. If you do it correctly you will feel your hand rise on your stomach. We often take shallow breaths just into our chest. Deep breathing will keep us calm and deliver more oxygen to our brains.

9. Ensure that you can be heard. Practise projecting your voice further. Don't shout, but aim to be heard further away. Networking events can often be noisy as they are full of people busily chatting and connecting. If you speak too quietly and your audience can't hear you, after asking you to repeat yourself once or twice they will lose interest and walk away from you.

10. Ensure you have fresh breath! Don't eat spicy food before a networking event. If you smoke, be aware that the smell of cigarette smoke on your breath and clothes can be very offensive to non-smokers. Always have mints at hand.

 Fast Fact

As a speaker, I've spent some time with a voice coach. A few sessions with a professional voice trainer can make a huge difference to your voice quality and confidence.

Modern manners

Like many areas in this book, etiquette and manners can cover a whole book in themselves but in our fast-paced lives we must not forget that they go a long way. What is the difference between manners and etiquette? Etiquette is a series of written rules on how one should behave in a certain situation. Manners are the outward manifestation of one's inner character.

"Etiquette tells us which fork to use. Manners tell us what to do when your neighbour doesn't."

For me, a crucial part of someone being memorable is how people treat me. I'm a strong, independent woman but I still value chivalry. If a man opens a door for me or helps me put my case in the overhead compartment on a plane, I'm not insulted, I'm flattered and thankful that his mother taught him good manners. Think about how you treat people when you are networking. Are you gracious and charming?

In case you missed charm class at school, here are my essential tips for gracious networking:

1. Introduce newcomers to conversations warmly, and take care that no one is excluded in conversations.

2. If you are at a networking event in your company then introduce members of your team in order of seniority.

3. Try to say something nice and interesting about the person as well as their name and job title, such as, "This is Amanda Page. She works in HR, and she's also just completed a marathon in under four hours."

4. If you are going to the bar or to get coffee, offer to get refreshments for others as well.

5. Do what you say you will do in a timely manner. If you tell someone you will pass them details of a business blog or a baking recipe, then make sure you do it quickly after the event.

6. Say thank you often. Thank someone for sharing information with you, thank them for spending time with you at the event, and thank them when they send you the baking recipe, or if they follow you on Twitter.

7. Don't gossip about business colleagues or other people at networking events or on social media. The more people you get to know, the smaller the world becomes!

8. Always keep your ears open for opportunities that will help others in your network. If someone makes a connection for you then thank them, even if it comes to nothing.

9. Don't email blast everyone after a networking event. If someone has given you their business card, ask them if it's OK for you to add them to your mailing list, and if someone you added unsubscribes don't be offended.

10. Don't monopolise anyone's time at a networking event. You may find them really interesting and they could be a brilliant connection for you, but they are at the event to network too, so give them the opportunity to exit from the conversation if they want to. Also don't just huddle and chat with your friends. It can make an event seem very cliquey and put off newcomers — remember that you too were a newcomer once.

Star Tips for making yourself memorable

1. Fake it until you make it. Walk into a room feeling like a celebrity and that everyone already knows and loves you. Eventually they will!

2. Pay attention to colour psychology. The colours you wear will affect your mood and also how you are perceived by others. Make sure your colour choice is right for the situation, your skin colouring and also that it conveys the right message.

3. Make sure that your clothes look like they have been purchased in the last five years. Forward-thinking successful people replace their clothes and keep up to date.

4. Be a bargain hunter but don't buy cheap, poor quality clothes unless you want to be perceived as giving a cheap, poor quality service yourself.

5. Cull your wardrobe and ensure that everything in it reflects how you want to be perceived.

6. Become aware of your own body language. Talk to yourself in the mirror and begin to recognise traits and inconsistencies. Banish any body language blunders you are making.

7. People-watch as often as you can. Sit on your own with a cup of coffee in a crowded coffee bar and study the body language of those around you. The better you can read the unconscious messages of others, the more effectively you will be able to build rapport with them.

8. Record your own voice and listen to it. Does it need work? Should you slow down or add more enthusiasm? Critique your own voice and take steps to improve any glitches.

9. Go back to charm school! Improve your manners. Become aware of when others exhibit bad manners, think of how they should have behaved and ensure that you never behave in the same way.

10. Be helpful and courteous to others but don't become a doormat. Keep track, either physically or mentally, of who is asking for what, and if someone oversteps then learn to say no.

ORGANISING FABULOUS NETWORKING EVENTS

"Even if you're on the right track, you'll get run over if you just sit there."

Will Rogers

So far we have been discussing what happens when you attend a networking event. In this chapter, I would like to take a look at the preparation you'll need to consider when hosting your own event. I've been holding and attending networking events for over ten years. I try to attend two networking events every week, so I've seen what works well and what is a recipe for disaster. I hope by sharing my experiences here, you will be able to avoid many of the mistakes I have made.

The first thing to do is carefully consider who to invite. What is the purpose of your event? Is it to bring together like-minded people who might do business with each other? Is it a social gathering to enforce relationships? Is it an industry event where people may actually be networking with competitors? Once you have clearly defined the purpose of your event, you will be able to research who to invite.

Here are some ideas of networking events that might inspire you to delve into your address book.

Networking to get new clients

In his book *Book Yourself Solid*, Michael Port talks about holding gatherings and networking events to bring in new clients. He tells a story of a personal trainer who holds 'healthy cooking' events once a month. His clients bring along cooking ingredients, and he shows them how to cook delicious, healthy food. His clients feel valued and enjoy the social interaction, and the events support the health and wellness of his brand. These events are free to all his clients, as long as they bring along a guest. The personal trainer uses these client networking nights to get a steady stream of new clients. Genius!

Networking to reinforce existing relationships

As an image consultant, my clients are my best advertisement. I have a vested interest in them continuing to stick to the rules that I have given them to dress with impact and style. Whenever one of my clients gets a compliment on their clothing, they will normally talk about me and how I helped them. To stay in contact with my clients I run regular events in a premium department store. Each event normally attracts over 150 of my clients and their friends. The department store closes early and stays open late, so the events have an air of 'exclusivity'. The store supplies canapés and wine. In return I bring them new customers who want to try and buy recommended clothes. At the event I deliver a 30-minute presentation in which I discuss the latest trends, which is a great value-add to my clients and a taster session for their guests. My guests then spend lots of money in the store, go home with fabulous clothes and enjoy a great networking night with their friends.

Let's look at all the benefits I see of doing this type of networking event:

- I give value-add and maintain the relationships with my existing clients.

- I meet lots of new clients.

- I create a great relationship with a premium department store.

- I make revenue from ticket sales.

Danger Zone

To charge or not to charge? I actually charge a small fee for some of my networking events. Experience has shown me that if my guests do not pay, even if it is a small fee, then they don't value the event and often don't turn up on the day. This causes logistical problems with the venue and catering.

Networking to win business

Premium hotels compete hard to win corporate business. Meeting rooms, seminars and visiting travellers make up a huge per centage of the revenue of any business hotel. Smart hotel managers know that the power often lies with the people who make the bookings, usually secretaries, administrators and personal assistants. I used to work with IHG Hotels in the UK to host some great networking events. The hotel would invite the bookers along for a fabulous afternoon tea. They would be served fresh strawberries and cream with a glass of champagne in summer, or mulled wine and marshmallows in winter. Lots of hotels do this, and often the bookers are too busy to attend these events, but by collaborating with me, IGH Hotels added extra value. By booking a speaker that the bookers might be interested in, their event became the 'must-attend' item in their calendars.

If the hotel invited bookers to come and have a cup of tea and see the venue, they might not come. When they invited them to come along to a talk given by an international image consultant about how to look younger, slimmer and maximise their business wardrobe, they made time and also invited their friends and colleagues.

Once the bookers are there, they are taken on a hotel tour and introduced to the staff and the facilities. In this way, the relationship between the hotel and the booker is reinforced.

Let's look at the wins in this scenario:

- The hotel staff get to meet the bookers personally.

- The bookers get to visit the hotel.

- The hired speaker either gets paid or has exposure to a large audience that may hire them in the future.

- The bookers feel valued and reassured that the hotel will take care of any guests they check into that hotel.

Try This

Brainstorm some ideas for networking events you could hold.

Who do I want to bring together?	Why? What is my desired outcome?	Ideas for the event

Administration for your events

As you are reading this book I'm going to assume that you are new to networking and have not run any networking events before, so I would like give you a few things to consider in terms of administration. First of all, where are your contacts? Is your event small and intimate, invitation-only, or the more the merrier? What information do you have about your prospective guests? Just their email address or all their contact details? You must consider this carefully before you plan your event. There is no point printing beautiful gold leaf embossed invitations to send out only to realise you don't have the postal addresses of most of your guests!

1. Sending invitations by post

We tend to receive so many invitations by email these days that when something arrives through the post it feels kind of special. I recently received a beautiful high quality invitation from the Australia and New Zealand Association inviting me to an awards reception and thanking me for being a valuable contributor in their programme. Did I feel special and that the event was a must? Absolutely!

I'd recommend postal invites for a very small number of guests.

Here are some things to consider when using traditional invitations:

- How will they RSVP? If that is important, then think about including a postage-paid slip or an email address so they can RSVP easily.

- It's probably not practical to send them a reminder by mail. Can you send them a reminder via email to follow up on your paper invitation?

- It could be more difficult to collate the RSVPs. People often forget to post them or some may get lost in the post. Will you be phoning them to chase their response? This can be very time consuming.

- How will you follow up after the event? Will you send them a thank you card? Lots more administration to consider.

I would recommend paper invitations for small, prestigious invitation-only events. The administration involved in such, as well as the cost, is considerable. Combine with email as well for the best results.

2. Sending email invitations

You could just create an email and send it to all your contacts. It's quick, easy and seemingly hassle-free, but let me share some additional tips on doing this.

Check the policy of your email provider. Some providers limit the number of recipients for each email. Some cap it at 50 or even as low as 30. If you exceed the limit, your email will be deemed as spam and your email account could be blacklisted. If you are using this very basic method, then make sure that you type the names in the Bcc field. This means that the other recipients do not see the names of all of the other recipients. It's terrible email etiquette to blanket email a list and reveal the other email addresses. You are exposing their email address to future potential spamming. If you decide to use email in this way be sure to send your emails in groups of 30–50 and ensure that the emails are in the Bcc field.

If you use Microsoft Outlook you can use mail merge to send individual invitations. I've given instructions below for Microsoft Office 2010. If you use a different system or different version, just consult the online help on how to do this with your email software.

Type the list of email addresses in a spreadsheet with their email addresses in one column and, if required, their names in another column. Save this file. In this example I will name my file 'Disney contacts'.

	A	B	
1	**Name**	**Email Address**	
2	Mickey Mouse	mickey@disney.com	
3	Donald Duck	donald@disney.com	
4	Daisy Duck	daisy@disney.com	
5	Pluto	pluto@disney.com	
6			
7			

Create a document in Word inviting your guests to the event.

Dear

I have pleasure in inviting you to our forthcoming networking event.

Come along, mix and mingle and meet other like-minded entrepreneurs.

Venue:

From the Mailings tab, choose Select Recipients and then Use Existing List.

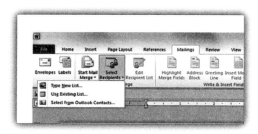

Here you will select the Excel file that contains the names you previously stored. You will be asked to confirm which sheet in the spreadsheet contains the email addresses, and then the files will be connected.

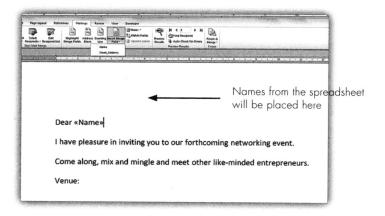

Names from the spreadsheet will be placed here

Dear «Name»

I have pleasure in inviting you to our forthcoming networking event.

Come along, mix and mingle and meet other like-minded entrepreneurs.

Venue:

If you have any fields from your spreadsheet that you would like to put in the email, you can use the Insert Merge Field button to place them appropriately.

Next click Finish, Merge and select Send E-mail Messages.

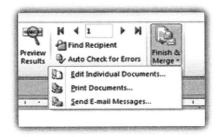 

If you have given your email field in the spreadsheet an appropriate name, then it will automatically be selected. Complete the subject line and then click OK. An individual personalised email will be sent to each recipient in your spreadsheet.

 Danger Zone

Be aware of the email spam laws in your country. Do you need to add in any extra words in bulk emails? In Singapore we must put <ADV> in the subject line. In other countries you may need to give the recipient the opportunity to unsubscribe and ensure thst you action the unsubscribe within 48 hours. Don't aggravate people you are trying to engage with by sending them unsolicited mail.

3. Use a CRM (Customer Relationship Marketing System)

If you work for a large company or association, you probably already have a great system that does this for you. However, if you are an SME (small and medium-sized enterprise) or an entrepreneur and you don't already have a CRM or mailing system, then you should seriously think about getting one. There are lots you can try, and many of them are actually free for a small amount of subscribers. I have used:

- Constant Contact

- Icontact

- MailChimp

- AWeber

All these systems manage your contacts. First you input all your contacts, and you can then easily send them newsletters, emails and surveys. You can also group or categorise your contacts into different lists or segments so you can selectively email them.

Whether you use one of these systems or you find a suitable alternative, there are many benefits of using a CRM mailing system:

- The system will take care of your unsubscribes. There will be a clear method of unsubscribing at the bottom of your email, and if the recipient clicks this link they will be permanently unsubscribed from your list.

- It will handle bounced emails, keeping track of emails that have not been delivered successfully so that you can investigate or delete them.

- Analytics will be provided. From this you can tell how many people have opened your message, how many times they read it or if they forwarded on or clicked on any of your links.

- There will be professional easy-to-use templates available to make everything very easy for you.

- Most CRM systems have social media interaction so you can easily promote your event on Facebook, Twitter, LinkedIn and other social media platforms.

- When you have created an event and added the list of recipients, it is easy to send reminder emails to all participants. You can also easily email just those who have signed up for the event, and follow up afterwards with those who attended or didn't attend.

Note: Once you reach a certain number of subscribers, there will be a cost involved with using a CRM system. I've only listed a few of the features and benefits of CRM systems. This type of system is a must for any business needing to build relationships with their customers.

Most CRM systems operate on option-only policy. Your recipients must have agreed to be part of your mailing list.

4. Facebook event

We will be looking at networking via social media in Chapters 8 and 9. Facebook events are a great way to promote an event if you you have followers or group members on Facebook. It's not the best way to manage your event, but it's certainly a great way to gain momentum for it.

Facebook allows you to create an event. There is an easy-to-use template that helps you select times and pinpoint your location. You can easily invite contacts from your Facebook account. You are able to invite people who are not your Facebook friends by entering in their email addresses, but they have to be on Facebook to be able to see the event. If you have a Facebook group, you can set up an event and invite all members of that group to your event.

There are many benefits of Facebook events:

- You can make your events public and let your guests invite their friends and colleagues too, so it's easy to attract huge numbers very quickly.

- The events are easy to set up and can be shared and promoted by all other Facebook users and posted to other social media platforms.

- You can easily see who is attending and not attending the event.

- You see a photo of most of the attendees, and you may be able find more in-depth information about many of them, including details of any mutual acquaintances, hobbies and interests. By doing research like this, you will be well ready for small talk.

- It's easy to send reminders and follow-up emails to all attendees or just those who have said they are attending.

- The guests can chat with each other and make comments before they attend the event.

- You can post photographs of the event afterwards for all the participants to view.

- If you encourage your guests to 'Check In' at the event, you can create publicity for your event as their friends will see where they are.

- It's very easy for guests to connect with each other after the event via Facebook.

- You can create a Facebook advertisement to promote your event online. Facebook advertising costs are very easy to monitor.

So with a very long list of benefits, why don't we use Facebook for all our events? Well, there are some drawbacks too:

- Not everyone is on Facebook. I still meet many people who are scared of the technology or just not interested in connecting via social media, particularly men.

- A lot of businesses prohibit the use of Facebook at work or limit the times it can be used. If your event is strictly business, then Facebook may not be the right tool to connect with your corporate market during working hours.

- You can't take any payments. If your event is fee paid, then the basic Facebook events page does not let you collect money so you will have to provide a link to another page or site where money can be collected. Of course, there are applications that you can integrate with Facebook to allow you do this, as well as Facebook pages modified by a technical expert.

- My biggest annoyance with Facebook events is that people don't take them too seriously. Many people click 'Join' to say they will attend the event, see the other people going, and then often just don't turn up. I hosted a networking event recently and 25 people said they were coming. Only five turned up!

- There is no way to print out a guest list. You would literally have to re-type the names.

- A Facebook event can be difficult to synchronise with the actual paid version of the event. Last week I turned up at a networking event, a pay-at-the-door event that I had accepted on Facebook. They wanted to turn me away as I had not registered on their system. Having been to a number of their events before, I had just skimmed through the details, saw that it was pay-at-the-door and clicked 'Join'. Way down in the text it mentioned that I was supposed to book online via their website.

5. Eventbrite

I'm going to mention an online event management portal called Eventbrite; I'm sure there are other competitors that do this job as well but my current favourite is Eventbrite. It completely manages everything to do with your event and it is practically free! Let me give you an overview of what it does.

- It allows you to create an attractive page for your event with very nice templates.

- It creates a Google map of the exact location.

- It allows you to post free or paid tickets, including early bird rates. You can also limit the number of tickets available at each price or free.

- You can send out invitations to names imported from a spreadsheet. Eventbrite currently also integrates with MailChimp.

- It takes PayPal or credit card payments. This is great, as a small business does not need to set up a complicated merchant account or deal with gathering cheques.

- You can still take payment at the door.

- You can easily post events to Facebook, Twitter and LinkedIn.

- It provides statistics of how many people have looked at your event. This is useful if you have sent out an invitation via email and want to check the responses.

- You can easily process refunds or allow the guests to cancel if you want.

- It prints your name badges.

- It prints your guest list.

- It automatically sends out e-tickets and reminders.

- You can also send additional emails to the participants whenever you want.

- It has a very cool system that lets you check in your guests at the door. You use an iPhone or an android phone to read a QR code on their printed ticket or displayed on their phone to quickly check them in.

- It will promote your event to other Eventbrite subscribers in your area if you wish. Your event can be public or private.

I've detailed some technology options that you might want to use to manage the administration of your event. Having had a wealth of experience in organising events, I can tell you that the administration can be a huge part and very time consuming, particularly if you are taking payments and checking membership details.

Fast Fact

When promoting an event, I've often found that you need to send out an email about the event on three separate occasions to get sign-ups. You may worry about bombarding people with too many emails, but think about how you respond to invitations when they come into your inbox. The first time you see it you may think "That looks interesting, I'll look at that later", then you forget about it. A week later you get another email and think, "Oh! I meant to take a look at that, I must do that later" and then probably only the third time nearing the event do you think, "Right I have to book before the places are full!"

Don't underestimate how much work it can take to administer a successful networking event.

Sending reminders to guests

Do send out a reminder for your event with clear instructions of how to get there, and alert the guests of any potential traffic issues. I used to run my department store events at 6.30 pm on a weekday in the centre of town. It was terrible for commuters trying to get into town when everyone else was leaving. I always advised them on the best routes to take and where to park cheaply and easily.

Depending on the event and the numbers attending, you may want to forward the guest list to all guests beforehand. I love it when this happens. You get to see who is coming and can often spot your big fish on the list and then look out for them at the event. It's often best not to include emails on this list in case of spam, but guest name, company name and a one-liner about them is great information to have for your guests. You can suggest that they print it out and bring it along, to save you from dealing with more administration.

Hiring a speaker

I touched on this earlier, but it can be a great idea to hire a speaker for your networking event. A lot of organisations run monthly events showcasing a speaker, and this can be a great incentive to attract a crowd. But how do you ensure the speaker is relevant to your audience? Will some people be put off if the speaker is not of interest to them? What happens if you book a speaker and they are not very good? How will that reflect on your event and future attendance? These are all things to consider.

If the event is arranged around a particular speaker, then most of the participants will be coming specifically to see that speaker. But what if your event is advertised primarily as a networking event with the speaker being the secondary attraction?

When I first moved to Singapore, I attended a Chamber of Commerce breakfast meeting. It had been how I previously grew my business and made many of my best friends, so I thought this would be the best place to start. The event was scheduled to start at 7.30 am and I arrived promptly, but very few other attendees arrived until around 7.45 am. At 8.00 am we were ushered into the ballroom for breakfast, and the speaker immediately started. The speaker presented for just over an hour, after which everyone quickly left to get to the office. There was absolutely no opportunity to network, only for ten minutes before the event. The speaker was terrible, not relevant to most of the audience, and difficult to understand. I sat there for most of the hour wishing he would hurry up and finish so that I could chat with the people on my table, but sadly he took up the whole hour. I didn't attend a breakfast meeting like that again.

If you are having a speaker, it is really important that the speaker is either specifically targeted to the interests of the group, or that there is plenty of time for networking. At most networking events I think the speaker should present for no more than 35 minutes to at least give the attendees the opportunity to discuss the event and network afterwards, both with the speaker and with guests.

It can often be difficult to check the credibility and skills of the speaker. I've sat through hundreds of terrible presentations. Bad presenters, terrible slides, even inappropriate or offensive content. How can you prevent that from happening? I was amazed that very early on in my speaking career, I could easily get booked for free talks without the organisers even talking to me or asking to see any testimonials from previous clients. I knew I could do an excellent job, but my hirers were leaving a lot to chance.

Here are some things to ask your prospective speaker before you agree to have them present at your event. As a speaker, I would expect to be asked these questions before taking a booking, even if it was a free one.

- How many years' experience have you had speaking?

- What audience sizes do you normally present to?

- How will you involve the audience in the presentation?

- What equipment will you need?

- Will there be any handouts for the audience?

- Can I see some testimonials from previous clients?

- Do you have any videos where I can see you speak? How will you tailor your presentation to be specifically relevant to the audience?

Danger Zone

Make it very clear that you are asking for a short presentation, not a sales pitch. Many speakers use free speaking slots as an opportunity to deliver ten minutes of content and a 25-minute sales pitch for their product or service. This is not what your audience has signed up for!

If a speaker is going to be a monthly focus of your networking event, then you could think about creating a theme for your regular events. Here are a few ideas for themed events:

Different types of events

1. Women-only events

A lot of women will be very nervous about attending networking events, particularly on their own. They will feel more comfortable if it's a women-only event. Women make excellent networkers as they can very quickly move into relationship-based conversations and are quick to build rapport. They often use networking events to make friends and grow their social circle. When one lady attends and enjoys the event, she'll tell all her friends and they will probably attend the next one. This type of event can grow very quickly and be very popular, and there will usually be a fun atmosphere. It's also easy to attract and choose speakers that are interested in marketing their product or services to women.

2. Business focused events

One Chamber of Commerce that I belong to runs business-themed networking events. We have the monthly marketing meeting, the monthly financial planning meeting and the entrepreneurs group. It's much easier to target the speaker specifically to the needs of the audience.

3. Hobby focused events

Create events within your organisation based on people's hobbies. For example, if you are the sports and social coordinator within a large company, perhaps you could create a photography group that would attract attendees from all areas of the business to network outside their normal work circle? They would enjoy any talk on improving their photography skills. Whether within a company or as a public event, hobby-based network events are a great way to meet new people.

 Aha! Moment

I can network while I am learning more about my favourite hobby or learning something new that seems totally unrelated to work!

4. 'Spray and pray' events

These are the type of events where you are probably inviting strangers. You are advertising your event through many channels, probably Facebook or even print advertising, and hoping for a huge crowd to turn up at the event. If they have not previously registered, you will need to collect their details. Have lots of clipboards and pens around so that people turning up to the event can give you their details. Have a prize draw (a bottle of wine will always do the trick) so that attendees take a moment to fill in their details. Take this opportunity to ask them a few important questions relating to your networking goals, for example:

- Can I add you to my newsletter list?

- Which of my services would you be interested in hearing more about?

- What problems do you have that my service or product could fix?

New technology gives you a great opportunity here. If you would like them to subscribe to a newsletter or be aware of a product or service, then give them the opportunity to scan a QR code. A QR code is a graphic that smart phones can scan that will then record details. Your guests could be storing contact details or be directed to a web page or Facebook page with a unique event offer. Think about it!

 Try This

Scan this QR Code and see where you end up!

 Fast Fact

Technology is making it easier for you to create and run your events and pass information to your guests. Make sure you keep up to date with what is available.

If you are running a 'spray and pray' type of event, it's a good idea to research websites that offer "what's on" pages. Contact local newspapers and magazines to see if they will advertise your event for free. Media needs information, and you'll be surprised at how much you can advertise for free.

5. Collaborative events

Are there other organisations you can collaborate with to introduce new contacts to your organisation or bring in new guests? In Singapore, the Australian Chamber of Commerce runs a huge event twice a year. Their Bi-annual Cheese and Wine Party is a major event. They hire the Asian Civilisation Museum and invite premium wine and cheese suppliers to hire exhibition slots in return for bringing crowds of eager wine drinkers and cheese enthusiasts. AusCham collaborates with the other Chambers and member organisations in Singapore and gives their members a special discounted rate; in this way they effortlessly attract hundreds of visitors and have their event advertised for free by partner organisations.

 Aha! Moment

If I collaborate with others for my networking event they can promote it to their database if I offer them a special rate or number of tickets.

Fee or no fee?

Firstly, think about the purpose of your event. If it is to bring you new clients, then it could be reasonable that you need to make a financial investment to get those new clients. If you are building relationships with existing clients or thanking them for being a loyal customer, then it would not be appropriate to charge for the event!

There are, however, some things to consider. I run a free ladies networking coffee morning called LadiesWhoLatte. We have no speaker, it's very informal, and it's a great starting place for anyone new to networking. Part of our appeal is that you don't need to book your place, you just turn up. It fits brilliantly into the lives of many women entrepreneurs, because if something comes up on the day of the event there is no hassle. You just don't go and no one is disappointed or let down. Of course, when something is free, it often has less value. I know that even if I charged a $10 registration fee I would get much higher attendance. Not because my ladies needed a return on investment on their $10, but because when you pre-pay for an event it puts you in a different mindset. People commit to attending and are more likely to honour that commitment.

Your return on investment

I just mentioned my networking group, LadiesWhoLatte (LWL). I started this group as an informal coffee morning in 2006 with just six ladies. LWL is now a global networking group with over 50 meetings every month, attracting over 7,000 ladies. It's still free to attend. LWL is run entirely by volunteers, some of whom work very hard and put in a lot of hours for their ladies. If I started LWL again I would definitely monetise it, not necessarily to make a profit but to be able to pay those involved for the considerable time they put in.

At the beginning of this chapter I detailed the huge amount of administration that can be involved in running networking events. Perhaps as an organiser of a number of events you need to be getting a return on investment for your time or at least breaking even on room hire and refreshments.

Running paid networking events could be an integral part of your business plan as it is in many associations, in which case you will most definitely need to charge. Think about how you will collect the money and what your policy will be for people who do not attend.

Star Tips for organising fabulous networking events

1. Define a clear purpose for your event. With a specific goal you will be able to assess whether your event has been successful afterwards.

2. Consider hiring a speaker to give a short presentation to give added value to your guests.

3. Ensure that there is always plenty of time for networking.

4. Send individual invitations via post, Facebook or other media to make each guest feel special.

5. Carefully plan how you will contact the guests, manage RSVPs and with guests after the event. Plan this sequence before the event rather than as you go along.

6. Send three reminders to attendees so that you get maximum attendance.

7. Familiarise yourself with social media channels such as Facebook to promote your event. Even if you are not inviting people via Facebook, it can be a great way to increase your brand awareness.

8. If it's a 'spray and pray' event, register your event with any online "what's on" guides and send out press releases.

9. If you decide to use Facebook, ensure that your guests are informed if they need to register or pay via a separate link.

10. Consider collaborating with other organisations to bring in more guests and get your event promoted to databases other than your own.

HOSTING A FABULOUS NETWORKING EVENT

"Success in life, in anything, depends upon the number of persons that one can make himself agreeable to."

Thomas Carlyle

7

The day has arrived. Your networking event is running and your guests will be arriving shortly. Are you ready for them? Be as excited about your event as if it were your birthday party. Your preparation, excitement, enthusiasm and energy will all be required to make the event a success.

Be as enthusiastic about your event as you would be if you were throwing a birthday party.

My tips here may seem obvious to some readers, but I've seen all of this done badly or not done at all, so I think it's definitely worth mentioning all this so you can avoid making the same mistakes.

Your role as the host

As the host, a lot of responsibilities rest on your shoulders. Depending on the size of the networking event, to do your job properly you will want to enlist a team of volunteers or even paid staff to help you. Your main responsibility as the host is to ensure that all the guests have a productive and pleasant event, as well as possibly achieving some of your own networking goals. This can be tricky and often stressful.

Unless it's a regular networking event with a small crowd, you'll really need to leave your personal networking goals at the door. At your event you must adopt the mentality of a host, with your major role being to take care of your guests.

Danger Zone

A networking event is not a party. When people pay to attend an event and give up their valuable time to come and network, they expect an event to be well planned and organised. As the host, you are responsible for this.

The registration process

It's important to have a printed guest list to check off your guests as they arrive. You must consider how to best arrange your list. For example, if you have groups of people attending from the same organisation, then list them in order of their company names. Guests from the same company often arrive together, so it's easier to find them and check them all in together. If your guests are not all coming from companies, list them by surnames and separate each letter of the alphabet with a heading clearly stating that letter of the alphabet. Sounds a bit silly but if you are the only person checking your guests in, and ten of them arrive at the same time, it's important to be able to register them as quickly as possible. People will often spot their name on a list faster than you can, so it will make it quicker and easier if you use a large typeface.

Eventbrite (mentioned in the previous chapter) has the coolest check-in process. Your guests print out e-tickets with a QR code on them, and as they arrive at the event you simply scan their tickets with your smartphone. If they have forgotten to print their ticket you can even scan their smart phone! Of course, you can check them in manually but this method is really quick and very impressive!

Always have a bowl at the registration desk for them to drop in their business cards. Give away something at your event, like a book, a bottle of wine, a box of chocolates — anything so that guests will more readily leave their cards with you. Collecting business cards lets you verify email addresses and contact details. People change jobs and email addresses frequently, so try and keep your contact list up to date.

Be careful where you drop your business card. I dropped my card into the bowl hoping to be in the prize draw. Half an hour later I found myself on stage in a beer-drinking competition! (I came in second.)

If you can enlist a person or people to help you with administration, then do so. Have someone else take money and deal with guests that have not registered. This way you can be the perfect host, greeting the guests as they arrive, welcoming them after registration and directing them to the main networking area.

 Fast Fact

Make sure you collect contact details. If you seriously want to grow your business by building and managing relationships, think of every contact you have as being worth $1. You'll value it more!

Name badges

Will you have name badges for your event? If so, are you going to prepare them in advance or simply give people sticky labels as they arrive? Preparing name badges in advance will make you look more professional, but it takes time. Eventbrite allows you to print name badges for your attendees easily before the event.

Danger Zone

Always have some blank name badges available for unexpected guests, substitutions or in case you have spelled someone's name incorrectly.

Pre-printing name badges also gives you another great opportunity to segregate your guests. Perhaps you have members and non-members. Give non-members or people new to the event a small sticker on their badge, eg a star, so they can easily be identified. Find a way to identify first-time visitors or VIP guests. Differentiate with different colour badges or stickers. One trick that I use when I want to be a little more subtle is to use a different font for people I particularly want to meet.

Another detail to consider is how your guests will attach the badges. Ladies wearing silk blouses may not want to pin their badge to their clothes with a safety pin. If your badge attaches with a clip, a lady wearing a blouse or a gentleman without a tie or pocket on his shirt would also have nowhere to attach the badge. Consider providing lanyards, but remember to collect them at the end of the event and re-use them to keep your costs down.

If you are a membership organisation then you could have badges created for your members. The best badges are attached by magnets so they don't ruin anyone's clothes.

Some organisations have credit card-style name badges that their members keep in their wallets. They can use these cards to gain discounts with partners and they also double up as name cards to slot into the name badge holders at the event.

Maximise your technology

If you have advertised your event and taken registrations via Facebook, encourage your guests to 'check in' via Facebook when they arrive. You migh have a small notice at the registration desk asking them to do so. The name of your event/organisation will then be advertised on their Facebook page to all of their friends. It's free advertising and brand awareness, so don't miss this opportunity!

Fast Fact

Think about every way you possibly can to advertise and promote your event so that you get more people to attend. If it's an invite-only event, it will be promoting your personal or organisation's brand.

Helping the flow of traffic

Once your guests have registered, you will want to help them to circulate and network. You won't always have control of the placement of food and drink, but if you do then spread it out. Have several food areas and several drink stations to ensure that your guests don't congregate in one area of the room. If your event is purely networking, don't have tables and chairs. Serve finger food that is easily eaten while standing. Get those great little attachments that you can put on the side of plates to hold a wine glass. It's impossible for people to swap business cards when they are holding both a plate and a wine glass. Alternatively, pedestal tables are useful so that standing guests can put down their plates or glasses.

If you are at a hotel or restaurant and you are serving food, appoint someone to keep check of the food levels. You don't want to be in the middle of a great networking conversation with someone, only to get interrupted because there are no forks. Delegate.

Host responsibilities

The most successful networkers will always adopt the host mentality. Even when you are a guest, work the room and behave like you are the host. However, as this really is your event, let me explain more about the host mentality and why it's ideal that you adopt it.

As the host, your main responsibility is to make sure that all the guests have a great experience at your event. Everyone will have their own reasons for attending and if you can find out more about why they are there and what they want to achieve then, as the host you can help them to have the best experience at your event.

It will depend on the size of your event, but you should try to greet each guest personally. If you know their names then greet them by name. They will be flattered that you remembered them from a previous event.

Let's dissect some sample conversations you might have, and glean some tips that you can take away.

Conversation #1 with someone you previously met

Host: "Hi Janice, Lovely to see you. So glad you could make it. You look fabulous. I love what you have done with your hair."

Shake her hand warmly, give her a big smile and use good eye contact. Greeting people by name is great, if you know it. Always thank people for coming, and remember that a compliment is always well received, not just by women.

Janice: "Thanks. I'm delighted to be here."

Host: "Great job on that article you had published in *HR Monthly*. I passed it on to a few of my friends. You raised some really good points there."

Smart networkers will follow what some of your networking contacts do by subscribing to their newsletters and following them on social media. You have to behave like a sponge. If you don't have a good memory, take notes and keep a record.

Janice: "Wow, thanks for that. I actually had some really great feedback. I'm glad you liked it."

Host: "Let me introduce you to Andrew. He's just published a book on leadership and I'm sure he'll be interested in some of the feedback that you received."

As the host, you have welcomed your guest and made her feel valued. Now add further value by introducing her to someone she will be able to chat with. That is so much better than that just saying, "Go network."

Host: "Andrew, Let me introduce you to Janice Shaw. Janice is the HR Director for ANC here in Singapore. She just wrote a fascinating article about Gen Y in the workplace for *HR Monthly*. Janice, this is Andrew Bryant. Andrew is just about to launch his second book on self-leadership, I'm sure you two will have a lot to discuss."

Introduce people with panache. Give them a lead, a hook, something to start the conversation with. By giving an introduction with a little more background, you are telling both guests that you know and value them.

Conversation #2 with someone you have not met before

Host: "Hello and welcome, David. I'm Sharon Connolly, the event organiser. I'm so glad you could make it today. There are already a couple of your colleagues from WWZ here today — Angela Collett and Gina Galvin. Do you know them?"

David: "Hi Sharon. Thanks for the invite. It looks like you have a great crowd here, and I see Angela in the corner over there."

I would know he is David from WWZ by looking at his name badge. If he doesn't know his colleagues, I have an opportunity to introduce him to people from the same company. If he does know them, then at least he will not be walking into a room full of strangers.

Fast Fact

At the beginning of the event, your role as a host is to meet the guests, make them feel welcome and then introduce them to someone else as quickly as possible.

Remembering names

How many times have you been introduced to someone only to forget his or her name as soon as you have shaken hands? Successful networkers need to sharpen their memory skills and learn how to remember names. Often, we 'forget' names not because we cannot recall them, but because we never stored them properly in the first place.

Imagine this scenario: I start a conversation with "Hello, my name is Sharon Connolly," returned with, "Nice to meet you. I'm Phil Derbyshire." There's nothing difficult about the names Sharon and Phil, but the problem is that while Phil is giving his name, I am thinking about what I am going to say next. The name is not set to memory, and I leave the meeting having no idea of who I just met.

In addition to being frustrating and embarrassing, forgetting names can end up costing you in your professional life.

Fast Fact

Business referrals, clients, customers and patients all want to feel valued. When you remember a person, calling him or her by name, you are showing that they matter to you. This also gives you an edge over your competition.

Let me share some tips to help you recall names.

1. Pay attention

You'd be amazed at how little attention we pay to the person we are meeting. Our eyes may be scanning the room for other people at the event or we may be nervous about what we are going to say next. Focus on the person and pay attention. Listen when your new acquaintance says his name. Clear your mind and focus on him — not on what you're going to say next.

2. Repeat the name you just heard. Say it right back to the person

Phil: Hi, my name is Phil.

You: Nice to meet you, Phil.

Try to use the name at least twice more in conversation. For example, "Phil, tell me, what challenges are you currently facing here working with the Singapore suppliers?" Or, "Phil, it was great to meet you, I'll give you a call later this week with the information I promised you."

3. Introduce the person to others

An excellent way to commit a name to memory is to introduce the person to one or two others. For example: "Phil, let me introduce you to

Amanda. Amanda this is Phil Derbyshire, he's currently on secondment troubleshooting some problems they have at the airport."

Using this pattern, I have repeated Phil's name at least five times. That will help me commit it to memory.

4. Ask for the spelling

If the name is not familiar to you — perhaps it's foreign or otherwise unique — ask for the spelling to reinforce your understanding and to confirm that you have heard the name correctly. If they are wearing a name badge ask if you can see how the name is spelled. Best not to use this when someone has introduced themselves as 'Bob' or 'John' though!

Many people are hesitant about asking for the spelling or just asking the person to say his name again. Don't be. People like it when you take an interest in them, and they are usually happy to repeat their name if it means you're actually going to remember it as well as other details about them.

If you work cross-culturally, you'll find that some people have really unusual names, or names that seem very unfamiliar to you. These people often have their names forgotten or mistaken. Imagine the impression you'll make when you take the time to truly understand their name, get the pronunciation correct and remember it.

5. Really study their features

Spend time discreetly studying someone's face. Notice distinctive features. Do try and look for the positives first. Has the person got amazing hair, a beautiful smile, crooked nose, a cleft chin, big ears? If possible, identify the feature before you're introduced so you're not struggling to find one while the person is giving you his name. Your brain will naturally associate this feature with this name.

Danger Zone

Focus on things that will be permanent. The lady with the great shoes may not be wearing great shoes the next time.

Myth Buster

If you think that you are just unlucky and don't have a good memory for names, then you are wrong. You can learn skills to vastly improve your memory. If you want to learn some practical techniques to remember anything, read *Maximise your Memory Power* by Nishant Kasibhatla, also in this Success Skills Series.

After the introductions

As the event progresses and you have greeted all the guests, it's important that you look out for the wallflowers and floaters. You will also want to rescue any new networkers who look like they are being monopolised by someone trying to sell to them. As you become more experienced and get to know people more, you will start to recognise great networkers as well as really bad ones. If someone new to networking does not have a great experience at one of your events, it can knock their confidence for a long time. Do everything that you can to help the new networker.

Appointing ambassadors

Consider appointing ambassadors to help you greet guests and handhold inexperienced networkers. The best ambassadors will be experienced networkers who can put guests at ease and welcome them. If you are a membership organisation, your ambassadors can also be briefed with information about the organisation and tell guests more about it.

Skilled ambassadors will also adopt the host mentality. They'll find out a little about the guest and then connect them to other guests in the room. This means the ambassador will then be free to connect with new guests.

Find some way for people to identify ambassadors. I love being an ambassador at my monthly Athena Network women's group. They attach a big pink feather to my name badge. The organisers know that I am a skilled networker and knowledgeable about their organisation, so I will be able to greet newcomers on their behalf.

Making someone an ambassador makes them feel special and helps take the pressure off you to deal with guests and less experienced networkers.

Try This

Write down who you know that is a skilled networker. Who can you enlist in your organisation to help you run successful events? Which of your friends or colleagues would be able to help you run your own events with more professionalism?

Managing your guest speaker

In the previous chapter we looked at the benefits of having a guest speaker to add interest and focus to the event. Let me share some tips to ensure that your speaker feels valued and that the audience gets the best service from the speaker.

- Prior to the event, you would have briefed the speaker about who will be in the audience. The speaker may then have the opportunity to tailor his presentation to your audience.

- Find out what equipment the speaker requires and have it ready in advance. You don't want to be running around searching for a flip chart two minutes before they are due to speak!

- If the speaker is bringing a presentation with him, make sure you know whether it's a Mac or PC, and whether his software will be compatible. You don't want to hear the words, "Well I just assumed you would have a Mac adaptor for the projector."

- Ideally the speaker should arrive well in advance of the event so that you can ensure that his presentation and audio (if any) works. If you can also delegate this to someone, they can be responsible for this on your behalf.

- I suggest that you brief your speaker not to deliver a long sales pitch. Giving details of a product or service at the end of the presentation is OK, but 30 minutes of selling never fails to get negative feedback from your guests.

- As the host, it's important that you introduce your speaker, or appoint an MC (Master of Ceremonies) to do this. Ask the speaker for a short biography and aim to introduce them in just two or three sentences.

- Ensure the speaker sticks to his allocated time slot. Have someone at the back of the room hold up signs for the speaker when they have ten minutes, five minutes and just one minute left.

- When the speaker finishes, the audience will normally applaud, and you must thank him. If you can pick one or two points from his talk and share with the audience how you particularly loved those points, this shows the speaker that you paid attention during his talk. Then ask the audience to applaud the speaker again.

 Aha! Moment

Delegating to a team is a crucial part of running a successful networking event!

Getting feedback

It is a great idea to get feedback from your guests on what they thought of your event. What did they love? What didn't they like? What could you do better? You won't know unless you ask them. If you have had a speaker and it's been a formal seated event, then give the audience feedback forms so that they can write down their comments. If it was a standing event, consider sending out feedback forms via email after the event, but remember that you'll probably only get a small percentage of those back via email.

One of the most valuable questions you can ask your guests to fill in on a feedback form is "Can you leave me a comment that I could use as a testimonial for future events?" Here you are asking permission and also gaining information that you can use in marketing material for future events.

If you receive any negative feedback, it's always wise to follow up with the guest individually. Even if it's is just an acknowledgement of their dissatisfaction, if you let someone know that their comments have been heard, they will feel more valued.

Following up

I've devoted Chapter 10 to looking at how you can stay connected, but when organising your event do consider if and how you will contact your guests afterwards. Will you send them a thank you email? If there has been a speaker, perhaps you can email to forward some notes or extra materials from the speaker. If your guests filled in a contact form, did you ask them if they wanted any additional information from you? If so, you may need to call them to provide additional information. You should be getting the hang of this now. Networking is about building and nurturing relationships, so always find ways to contact people after any event.

Star Tips on hosting a fabulous event

1. Appoint ambassadors to greet guests and facilitate networking throughout the event.

2. Delegate as many tasks as you can so that you are free to skilfully schmooze.

3. Collect business cards and hold a prize draw so that you can easily get the details of attendees and check that your contact details are current.

4. Plan sign-in sheets carefully so that you can quickly and easily register your guests on arrival.

5. Ask your guests to check in at your event on Facebook to create a buzz about your event.

6. Code the name badges so that you can easily identify new contacts or hot prospects.

7. Set up the room so that the guests are encouraged to move around and mingle. Avoid seated events if pure networking is your focus.

8. Communicate with speakers beforehand to ensure they know what is expected, and so you can be well prepared for them on the day.

9. Ensure that speakers keep to their timeslot by having someone alert them when their time is nearly up.

10. Find a reason to contact your guests again, perhaps by sending them a newsletter or a presentation, anything so that you continue the conversation.

THE NAKED NETWORKER: NETWORKING ONLINE WITH FACEBOOK

*"Facebook is like a fridge.
Even though you know
there is nothing new going
on you may feel the need to
check it every ten minutes."*

Unknown

8

Be careful not to have the webcam switched on if you are naked networking!

I find it hard to believe that we've only had the Internet since 1995. I remember my husband, who was a technical nerd, speaking via his computer to other technical nerds late at night. I made those disapproving tutting noises that only wives, mothers and teachers can do, thinking, "Computers talking to each other — whatever next? Who would have the time or the inclination to sit chatting to each other in front of a screen?" How fast things change!

Today, Google has reached the coveted brand panacea earned by brands such as Coca-Cola and Hoover, where their name becomes the name for the product. We don't order a glass of Cola, but a Coke, we don't vacuum the carpet, we Hoover it. And we don't search for something on the Internet, we Google it.

7.2 billion pages are viewed on Google every day by 620 million browsers. One in eight people who got married in the USA last year met online. We chat online, buy online, research online and we can even watch TV online. So it's important to network online too.

Like a world without the internet and a world without Google, I find it hard to imagine a world without Facebook. I do still meet people who are not on Facebook, for their own valid reasons. However, if you hope to become more successful via networking, you cannot underestimate the power of social media to network and connect with others, particularly if you want to grow your network globally.

There are comprehensive manuals for every type of social networking application. It would be foolish to give too much detail about all the ins and outs and technical aspects of any social media platform. Instead, we'll look at an overview of the most popular sites, and I'll share some pointers on how you can use them to network.

Fascinating Facebook facts

Let's look at some interesting facts about Facebook (as at June 2012):

- 955 million monthly active users.

- Approximately 81 per cent of these monthly active users are outside the US and Canada.

- 552 million daily active users on average.

- 543 million monthly active users who used Facebook mobile products.

These users spend an average of 6 hours and 33 minutes on the social network each month. Twitter, Tumblr, Instagram and the up-and-coming digital pinboard site Pinterest, may all be growing in popularity, but they clearly can't compete with Facebook in terms of attention and engagement.

Danger Zone

Ignoring technology can be a disaster for networking. Not only will you miss out on invites to events, you will miss out on the pre- and post-event networking.

Your Facebook dilemmas

I'm a huge Facebook fan. I connect with my friends and family all over the world via Facebook. I live my social life through events posted on Facebook. More importantly, I use it as a valuable tool in business to connect with my existing customers and to generate new business.

As much as I love Facebook, when networking for business it creates a number of dilemmas. You will need to think about these too.

In the early days of Facebook I was living in the UK, and it was easy for me to draw the line on who I accepted on my Facebook page. Facebook was strictly for close friends and family. Clients and business associates were invited to connect with me on LinkedIn. This worked perfectly and I stuck to that rule stringently. When I moved to Singapore, however, it became a lot more difficult. I had no friends. It was easier for me to meet new people through business connections. These new contacts started to request connections on Facebook and I was then faced with a predicament. I wanted to connect with my new contacts, to stay in touch, to build better relationships with them, but these were new contacts. Did I want to them see pictures of me playing on a beach with my children, or drinking in a bar with my friends? You need to ask yourself similar questions too.

Facebook fundamentals

Just in case you have been living under a rock for the last few years and you have not yet used Facebook, let me first explain some fundamentals. These may also be useful if you have some pre-conceived ideas about it and have decided that it's not right for you. Perhaps a little more research and reading will make you better informed, especially if you are keen to network.

1. A Facebook profile

First you create a Facebook account. You populate your account with information about yourself. You decide how much you want to share — you can fill in as little or as much information about yourself as you would like. You may share:

- Your age.

- Who is in your family.

- Where you work.

- Where you went to school.

- What interests you have in terms of hobbies and recreation.

- You have something called a 'timeline'. On your timeline you can choose to post status updates about things that interest you or that are going on in your life. You can share photographs, videos, links or just write text. You post these status updates, and your friends can also post updates on your timeline.

- You can play games with other Facebook users.

- Users post events such as meetings, parties and gatherings, and invite other Facebook users to attend. Guests can see who is going to these events.

- You can create photo albums and share these photos with other Facebook users.

Other Facebook users connect to you as friends and you get to see information about their profiles too. An intensive user of Facebook imparts a lot of information.

When you accept someone as your 'friend' on your personal profile, they will be able to view information about you, and vice versa. When they write comments on their profile, add photographs, attend events and generally interact in any way with Facebook, you will also be updated. How? Well, you'll be able to see all your friend's activity on their Facebook profile, and they will be able to see yours. But there are detailed security options too, so that you can restrict who sees what, and you can also decide which friends you would like to see updates from. We'll look at this a little later in this chapter.

 Aha! Moment

I can use Facebook to connect with others and still retain a high level of personal privacy.

2. A Facebook page

The main difference between a profile and a page is interaction with other Facebook users. Unlike your Facebook profile, where connections 'friend' you, on your business page they will 'like' you. When someone 'likes' your page, you don't connect with them in the same way as you would if you were Facebook friends. Their profile can still be marked as totally private and you will not see any of their activity. They can see all the activity on your page and will get updated when you post items, but you will not know anything about them, unless of course they are a friend too. Although you can have more than one administrator for a Facebook page, the posts on the page are generally driven by the owner of the page, with your fans adding comments and interacting. As the page owner, you can limit what others may post on the page.

Fast Fact

There is currently no way to send an email to all the members of your page. You can write a post and hope that your fans see it, but you cannot contact them all directly in any way.

3. Facebook groups

Another area of Facebook you need to be aware of is a Facebook group. A group can be set up for people to collaborate on a common theme or topic. The group can be open so that anyone can join, or it can be private where members are added by invitation only.

Members of a group can participate in discussions, post comments, ask questions and generally interact with each other. The group administrators can create events and easily invite all members of the group to the event. The group administrator is able to contact all the members of the group directly via email to their Facebook message inbox.

Fast Fact

Let me summarise:

- Your profile is where you share your personal information with other Facebook users who are termed as 'friends'. Friends can interact freely with each other and share personal information.

- A page is set up by a business or location. Other Facebook users can 'like' the page. The content is driven by the page owner, and fans can see the information and comment on it.

- A group is set up by an organisation or individual. Others are invited to join the group. Groups encourage active communication from all participants.

Using Facebook to network

Facebook can be a great networking tool. However, you do need to think about your own usage policy. For example, if you work for an organisation, will you add your work colleagues as friends? If you do, should you limit what they can see? You need to decide what is right for you to post and reveal to others. My personal view is that I never post anything that I wouldn't be happy for my mother to see. I do, however, have a pretty lively group of friends and a fast-paced life, so if my job was in corporate law then I may have to rethink that strategy. I won't detail here exactly how to change your settings, as the procedures and options change all the time. However, do remember that you can restrict who sees what at any time so that you maintain your privacy on Facebook if you want to, while still using it to connect with others.

Networking is about building relationships with others. It's often about getting past the 'What do you do for work?' questions and really getting to know people as people. Facebook gives you an insight into lives. You see families, homes, holidays and hobbies. You get to see a snapshot of a person's life, in full colour in pictures, very quickly. This helps you to build relationships and move to common ground very much faster than would normally be possible.

If I meet someone new and then connect to them on Facebook and find that they have been on holiday to an exciting location, then the next time I see them I have a great conversation opening. "How was your holiday? The beach looked amazing, and I saw that you went white water rafting." Or, "I saw a picture of your dogs on your profile. They are delightful. I have a Labrador too."

Your personal profile

If you decide to be a very private person, you will probably not be the most successful networker. People like people; real people with real lives, real hobbies, real problems, issues and ideas. People like people who are like them, so if you don't let anyone know anything about you then how will they know how they can help you or how you can help them? My Facebook profile gives snapshots of my life. I post things about my work, my social life, the odd picture of my children, my dog and a lot of me and my friends having fun. I'm aware that some of the people who are my 'Facebook friends' do not know me that well, so I do limit some of the content of pictures and posts, but it still allows me to connect and interact with a large group of people. For example, for one of my courses I was interested in working with a nutritionist and a personal trainer. I wrote a post asking if anyone had worked with either, and within a few minutes I had some referrals.

Let's take a look at the networking wins that could happen from a single post. When I ask if anyone knows a good nutritionalist, Harriet, one of my Facebook friends, sees my post. As my name pops up, she's reminded that she meant to book my eight-week course, so she makes a booking. She also recalls that she knows a nutritionist, and she messages me with a recommendation. A referral and recommendation from someone you trust is very powerful. I can now confidently contact the nutritionist knowing she comes highly recommended.

Harriet just thought of her friend Ellen the nutritionist, whom she hasn't spoken to for a while, and she drops her a quick email asking how she is, and mentioning that she has just passed on a referral. Ellen appreciates the referral, and she reconnects with Harriet. Ellen also watches out for the email coming in from me, and deals with the enquiry swiftly and professionally because she wants to ensure that she does a great job so that Harriet recommends her again. One little Facebook message and two people who might not have connected can do business together, and both are very appreciative to Harriet, who went out of her way to help, and we wonder how we might help her in the future.

I also have to highly recommend Facebook for allowing me to continue to network globally and gain opportunities that I never would have dreamt would be open to me as an international speaker. Facebook was fairly new when I left the UK in 2009. I used it purely to connect with friends and family, and my business contacts were all directed to stay connected to me on LinkedIn. However, Facebook grew in popularity among business owners, so there was a pressure for me to accept some of these networking contacts as friends. As I was leaving the UK, this seemed a great way to stay in contact with people and also to share my new experiences in Singapore. At that time there were no business pages, so I added quite a lot more UK contacts onto my personal site.

When I arrived in Singapore I started adding my new contacts as friends, and I was astounded by the mutual friend connections. I'd add a person I met as at a networking event and we'd find we had a mutual friend or even several. Someone who interviewed me for a job at a finance company went to school with one of my best friends from the UK. A client messaged me asking for advice to help a friend visiting Singapore, wondering if I could have a chat with them about what it was like to live here.

 Fast Fact

Mutual friends and a desire to help other people selflessly starts conversations and builds trust and rapport very quickly.

My views on what you should put on Facebook are quite different to those of many social networking experts. I hear stories of 40 per cent of job applicants being turned down because of improper social media postings; stories of people being fired for defamatory comments about their boss. I feel sure many of these are urban legends. If someone is the type of person to make defamatory comments about their boss, if they were not writing it on Facebook then they'd most likely be making those comments somewhere else where they would be heard. I asked many HR professionals if they checked the Facebook profiles of their job applicants, and "never" or "rarely" were the answers. Perhaps at a later stage in the interview process, but not early on.

I have also interviewed many senior hiring managers of global companies to ask about their attitude to seeing people drinking alcohol on their Facebook profiles. Most of them said they were likely to worry more if the person was not seen socialising and having a good time with their friends. People hire people who will fit in well with their teams. It's a rare team-building and networking event that runs in the evening and does not serve wine. Out of all the evening networking events that I attend in Singapore every month, only one of them does not serve alcohol.

Danger Zone

It's OK for your work colleagues to see you with a glass of wine. Dancing on a table semi-naked while drinking gin straight from the bottle on the other hand, perhaps not!

Things not to do on Facebook

- Don't over-post. People do not need to know what you had for breakfast, lunch and dinner.

- If you wish to connect and network with a varied audience, you must be careful about expressing political or religious views that may be offensive.

- Don't insult or disrespect the company where you work or your boss or colleagues. It will come back to haunt you.

- Do not allow others to post pictures on your timeline without first approving them.

- Create a balanced profile. It's fine to show yourself having a great time out at a party, but balance it with some information about what a great job you did with a recent presentation.

Danger Zone

If you post something sensational, be aware that it has the ability to go viral within minutes. It could get you into a lot of trouble.

If you post too much information, or if you keep posting silly "It's raining again" remarks, you will probably find that people will delete you from their news feed and then they will never know when you post interesting information.

Your professional Facebook page

This is an example of my Facebook page today. I'm using it very effectively to win business and network with a larger client base. Let me share how.

At the time of writing I have 1078 fans. These are people who are genuinely interested in what I do. I could easily source thousands of fans through third party vendors, but these would not be real fans. Real fans follow you because of the content on your site. They interact with you and create a buzz and a discussion. Many of my fans are actually friends whom I also know personally.

I post recommendations for clothes. I find bargains and provide solutions to my fans' dressing dilemmas by posting collages of recommended purchases. I talk about make-up products and also post some how-to videos. My fans interact with me and also with each other, so we're all networking — online.

How does it help me? When I attend a networking event, people who have met me have something to talk to me about. It also keeps me 'top of mind' because when someone asks them if they know an image consultant I would immediately come to mind. When I created an eight-week image course, I had 40 registrations, mainly friends and friends of friends who were connected to my company page. People who were unable to attend recommended it to others. My Facebook activity translated into actual business revenue and increased my networking relationships. Another great thing about online networking is that we can often actually see the communication trail, whereas with person-to-person networking we are sometimes unclear where our referrals come from.

Facebook now has a very sophisticated advertising system. When I create a post or story on my Facebook page, I have the ability to easily advertise that post to my target audience. Because Facebook knows so much about so many of its users, as an advertiser you can target your advertising spend very wisely. I can promote a story on my page, the page itself or send interested users to a page outside of Facebook. Whatever my desired outcome, I can create more attention or brand awareness by advertising, which can be useful in making connections.

Shortly after I arrived in Singapore I went to my first meeting of Asia Professional Speakers Singapore (APSS) . As an aspiring speaker, I was nervous and not sure what to expect. I recognised Shirley Taylor, the series editor of this book, from an advertisement I had seen about her business, and I had followed the link to find out more. When I saw Shirley at the APSS event, I had something that I could talk to her about. I introduced myself and told her I had seen her advertisement and liked her website. I'm sure she was pleased to know that her advertising was actually working, and everyone likes to hear good things about their website. I also complimented her on a lovely dress she was wearing that evening, and she gave me the details of the tailor who had made the dress. I later contacted Carol, the tailor, and we went on to work together quite extensively. Shirley and I also developed a friendship. We work together frequently and even occasionally share a glass of wine!

 Aha! Moment

Through Facebook I can create great new friendships, and make some great business contacts too.

Facebook groups

In terms of pure networking possibilities, a Facebook group is your most powerful online networking tool.

There are currently 140 members of Asia Professional Speakers Singapore. We hold monthly meetings and other ad-hoc events, and we are a welcoming, friendly environment for both professional and aspiring speakers and trainers in Singapore. We have an amazing Facebook group with 492 members at the time of publication of this book.

Being part of this friendly, active group is a must for any speaker or trainer wishing to develop their skills, learn more about speaking and training, and network to win more business. Let me share some of the things we achieve in our Facebook group.

- We promote events to existing and potential members and guests.

- We post photographs of previous events.

- Members and guests who attended each session post great feedback about our events, which interests others who may not have attended before.

- We warmly welcome and interact with new members of the group.

- Our members post their accomplishments. If someone wins a great new job, they share information. This motivates some of the new and aspiring members.

- Members ask questions and get valuable feedback from other members. Speakers who contribute are positioning themselves as experts in their field with valuable experience. Lots of issues are posted here, from ethical dilemmas to technical issues and supplier enquiries. Answers come in quickly, again leading to a win-win solution.

- I benefit greatly from collaborating with other speakers and trainers, as well as from their referrals to clients. Being active on this group again ensures that I am 'top of mind'!

- When a new member attends our networking event, they will recognise active contributors to the Facebook group. Existing members can identify new members and provide a warm welcome.

- New and prospective members can immediately see that we are a great association to join if they want to grow a speaking and training business, or network with others who are doing the same.

Aha! Moment

I can network with members of groups that I don't even formally belong to.

Facebook events

Become an active group member, and people will be clamouring to meet you.

Such is the popularity of Facebook that many organisations now forgo other ways of advertising events and post purely on Facebook. If you are not active on Facebook, you may miss out on great opportunities for networking events too. When you accept an invitation to an event on Facebook, you will normally get to see who else is attending. This can be an excellent opportunity to research the other guests and find out who your big fish may be.

In the lead-up to the event there may be discussions and posts that you would miss out on if you did not have access to the Facebook events page.

After the event, the Facebook event page can be a valuable resource for you to find details of people you met there, and to share thoughts or initiate discussions with the other attendees.

After you have clicked 'Join' to say that you are going to an event, make a comment on the page so that your profile name and picture are more visible to other attendees. When you attend the event, click to 'check in' through your mobile phone. This way your friends and colleagues will see you are out working hard to grow your business, and mixing and mingling with the movers and shakers! Other people at the event will see your name when they check in too. It's all great for exposure!

 Danger Zone

Facebook can be a powerful networking tool. If you choose not to use it you are potentially missing out on huge opportunities to network online.

Star Tips on using Facebook to network

1. Sign up and get a Facebook profile today, if you haven't already got one.

2. Examine the Facebook profile and security settings carefully, and understand how you can restrict who sees what. Pay special attention to the setting that makes sure that you approve other things that people can post with your name in it.

3. Make a conscious decision on your own personal Facebook policy. Decide who is appropriate for you to connect with and what they will be able to see – this will depend on your job.

4. Separate your business or public persona by creating a Facebook page, if appropriate.

5. Search for groups that network in your area and join them. This way you will be notified of any events they are holding.

6. Join discussions in groups that you are a member of. It well help get you recognised at events.

7. Seek out pages of companies and individuals that you admire, and join the discussions there. Everywhere your name and picture is displayed, it is exposure and a chance to make new connections.

8. Always officially 'Join' an event and 'check in' at the event to publicise yourself to other guests.

9. Post any work accomplishments on your profile. Success is 30 per cent ability and 70 per cent visibility, so let everyone know how hard you are working. It could be just what you need to balance out some of your partying!

10. Adopt the giving mentality on Facebook. If someone asks for help and you can help them, do it! Go out of your way to connect people together who can help each other.

SOCIAL MEDIA BEYOND FACEBOOK

9

"How can you squander even one more day not taking advantage of the greatest shifts of our generation? How dare you settle for less when the world has made it so easy for you to be remarkable?"

Seth Godin

In the last chapter I focussed purely on Facebook. Many people spend more time networking on Facebook than anywhere else, but there are other places you can go. You need to network where your audience hangs out. If you are trying to connect with a corporate audience, LinkedIn would be a better place for you to network online. If you play in a band and want to get more fans along to your gigs, you'll be better off uploading your music and starting conversations on MySpace. Like face-to-face networking, you need to focus on your goals and find out where your target audience hangs out.

 Fast Fact

In online technology, things move fast! YouTube was founded in February 2005 by three ex-PayPal employees. Such was its growth and social networking potential that Google purchased it just 18 months later for $1.65 billion. You need to constantly be on the look out for the next 'new' thing and jump aboard quickly.

Let's look at some of the other social media platforms where you can connect with others.

Pinterest

Pinterest, as described by Wikipedia, the free online encyclopedia, is a pinboard-style social photo-sharing website that allows users to create and manage theme-based image collections such as events, interests, hobbies and more. Users can browse other pinboards for inspiration, 're-pin' images to their own collections, or 'like' photos. Pinterest's mission is to "connect everyone in the world through the 'things' they find interesting" via a global platform of inspiration and idea sharing.

The phrase that should make you sit up and take notice there is "connect everyone through the things they find interesting". Entrepreneurs will post things about their businesses, and corporate employees may simply post details of a speaker they heard recently that inspired them. Whatever they post is a gem for you as an enthusiastic networker as it gives you something to talk to them about. Find out if people in your network have Pinterest boards and keep up to date with their boards. Post comments so that they are aware you are interested in them and if relevant share information if it can help them.

Is Pinterest here to stay, or is it a flash in the pan? Well in 2012, Pinterest won best social media app and people's voice award at the Webby Awards for best functioning visual design. Major retailers have started to display the Pinterest logo on many of their sites, enabling users to quickly and easily pin images from their sites to their Pinterest boards. So it looks like it may be here to stay.

I was working with a client recently who had just opened a furniture store in Singapore. She knew that social media was going to be a very important tool for her to grow her business but she was very unsure, and scared about how to do this. She was already overwhelmed by the number of social media platforms there were, so she sort of freaked out when I mentioned Pinterest! However this is probably the most useful of all the social media tools she could use to grow her network.

As an interior designer, she can use Pinterest boards to create gorgeous room settings. She can pin pictures of her furniture on the boards and so much more. If she collaborates with other suppliers, such as soft furnishing suppliers, she can also promote their products to compliment hers. She's establishing herself as an expert designer. She's collaborating with other complimentary businesses. She's giving valuable advice to others interested in interior design, and she's growing her client base.

When she has completed a Pinterest board she can easily post it to her Facebook page or Twitter account. She could even just print it out and create a great 'Look Book' for people who come to her store. When they see this they may decide to follow her Pinterest boards too. Again, it's about being 'top of mind'.

Fast Fact

Pinterest is like an idea board. You can share your visions with others!

LinkedIn

LinkedIn was founded in 2002 and launched in 2003. It now has over 175 million users in 200 countries. Its sole purpose was originally professional networking and its concept is based on the theory of six degrees of separation. You can connect to anyone in the world through a link of seven people that know each other. Here are some of the main features of LinkedIn:

- LinkedIn allows users to create a list of connections with whom they have some level of relationship. For me, the main power and purpose of the site is that I truly only connect with people that I know and have networked or worked with. I do get lots of requests for connections from people that I don't know, but I normally reject their request as I want my list of connections to be authentic. If someone asks me for an introduction to one of my connections, I want to be able to truthfully recommend them, which I can't do if I don't know them.

- Once you are connected with new people you can look through their list of connections and ask for an introduction. When you add a connection, you are alerted of mutual connections so you can consider who do they know that you know. It's a brilliant way to extend your network through mutual introductions.

- LinkedIn is like your online CV. You load details of your previous work experience and previous employees, and design your profile to showcase your work and community experience.

- Based on your skills, LinkedIn can recommend jobs that you might be suitable for.

- Employers post jobs and can search profiles for potential candidates. Recruitment consultants use LinkedIn extensively to headhunt and check out potential hires.

- Job seekers can review the profiles of hiring managers and discover which of their existing contacts can introduce them.

- Users can post their own photos and view photos of others to aid in identification.

- Users can now follow different companies and get notifications about the new job offers available.

- LinkedIn Answers is a forum area of the site where users post questions and other users can comment and provide insights and answers. This can be a great opportunity for you to position yourself as an expert or influential thought leader on a subject.

- Users can form LinkedIn groups similar to Facebook groups where they can interact with each other.

- LinkedIn recently allowed advertising. You can place an advertisement that specifically targets a LinkedIn demographic. LinkedIn has membership levels, and free users are not able to see as much information as those who pay. Names and contact details are limited for those who wish to use the site for free.

So that is a little bit of background on LinkedIn and why you might want to use it. Here are my top tips on how you can use it to network successfully:

1. Create a full and detailed profile

This is your online CV. List your accomplishments, your work history and any achievements you have made in your career. If necessary, get a professional to write this for you. It is important.

Fast Fact

If you are serious about job hunting and connections at a senior level, get a professional to write your LinkedIn profile for you. LinkedIn is a key tool used by head-hunters.

2. List every job and every position within that job

When you write your resumé, you might choose to leave out short contracts and temporary positions but recruiters will often search for people who have worked at a particular company and networkers might search for ex-colleagues. If you don't include the information you run the risk of not being found and missing out on a valuable connection.

3. List your achievements

When you write about your position, write about achievements rather than a boring list of responsibilities. If possible use statistics or evidence of real results, such as "By using new technology to streamline our order processing, I was able to cut order processing time by 25 per cent and reduce the cost of overheads by 20 per cent".

4. Get as many connections as possible

It will be your personal choice if you want to limit your connections to people you actually know, or are willing to accept all contacts, but whatever your choice do find as many connections as you possibly can. The LinkedIn search engines will view you more favourably the more connections you have.

5. Complete the skills section

The skills section lets you add keywords. These are the words people will use to find you, so do complete them in detail. You could go through job postings looking for commonly used words and phrases in your industry or profession because these are often the terms recruiters will search for.

6. Edit job title

The sub-header is visible in search results, ensure that yours is descriptive and engaging. When you enter your current job title, LinkedIn automatically places it underneath your name on your profile. You can use more than one line; it won't truncate it!

7. Create a personal URL

When you create a profile, LinkedIn will automatically assign you a profile URL that can be used to access your profile directly. This URL will have a combination of random letters and numbers. Change it to reflect your actual name if you can, or a variation of your actual name. Then when you pass it on to others it will be easier to use, especially if they have to type it in.

8. Ensure that your profile is public

As you are reading this book I'm assuming you want to network and connect with as many people as possible, so ensure that your LinkedIn profile is public. LinkedIn profiles feature high in the search engines when someone types in a name. If your profile is not public it will not be listed there.

9. Collect recommendations

Collect as many recommendations as possible. If you complete a project well, or work for a client that is delighted with your services then ask for a recommendation. Prospective contacts can read these and it is a great way for you to showcase them.

If you are serious about networking, you need to be very visible and active online.

LinkedIn recommendations are verified as being written by real contacts and connections so they really do carry weight. When I'm asked to submit information for a project and provide a recommendation, I don't have to go back to my clients and ask them for permission. I can just refer my prospective customer to my LinkedIn profile where they can see the evidence.

10. Reciprocate!

If you work with someone who has done a great job, write them a glowing recommendation. Your name will show on their recommendations and can attract more visitors to your profile if they click on your name. Associate yourself with great people and compliment them with a recommendation, and they may well then write one for you too!

11. Answer questions

'Questions' is an area of the site where you can position yourself as an expert and gain more exposure. Here you can provide answers to questions in your area of expertise. After someone posts a question, they need to vote on who answered it best. Giving the best answers to questions increases your credibility and also gives you the opportunity to network with other professionals in your field.

12. Join group discussions

Just like Facebook groups there are Linkedin groups. Join groups in your areas of professional expertise and comment and contribute regularly to be 'top of mind'.

Aha! Moment

With a little work you can make yourself an authority on a subject and become influential within a group of people all over the world. That's powerful!

13. Post projects

If you have worked on an interesting project within your organisation, or if you are a freelancer or entrepreneur who has worked with a great company, post your accomplishment as a project. When you write your resumé it can be difficult to recall all the great mini-projects you have worked on — keep adding them to LinkedIn so you can keep track of what you have done and who you worked with.

14. Post status updates

LinkedIn allows you to post status updates. What are you doing? What are you working on? Post regular status updates to ensure you are shown in the news feeds. These updates can automatically be posted on Facebook and Twitter to again keep yourself 'top of mind'.

15. Keep up to date

Like all the other social media platforms, LinkedIn constantly adds new features. Make sure you check out what is new and make use of it.

16. Go premium

Consider upgrading your account. By having a premium account other contacts know that you take your networking seriously. For a small monthly fee you can upgrade your account which will allow you to send emails (InMails) directly to people you would like to connect with. There will also be a small logo next to your name in a list of search results, which will show that you are a premium member.

17. Get a good profile picture

Here are some tips for getting a great corporate shot:

- Think carefully about where you might use the photograph and plan your shots accordingly. For LinkedIn ideally you want a great close-up headshot, but for magazines and if you have a website you might want something full length. Be appropriate for your job. My job is about fashion so its more appropriate for me to have a shot showing what I am wearing rather than a cropped headshot.

- Wear plain colours — stripes, spots and patterns might detract from your face. Avoid neutral skin-tone colours such as beige, peach or pale pink especially if you are using a white background. You are aiming for contrast.

- Avoid fussy jewellery. It will detract from your face, which should be the focus of the photograph.

- Wear a colour that makes your eyes stand out. Black is not the most flattering colour for most complexions, so consider navy, brown or charcoal grey instead.

- Think about the longevity of your photograph. Your photograph may be used all year round in countries with varied climates. Consider whether wearing a woolly jumper or a sleeveless top would be the right image all year round.

- Keep the styling classic rather than fashionable. You may be using your photograph for a number of years. You don't want to make it too obvious that it's a particular fashion era. That said, you do need to look current and I recommend getting new photographs every three years at least.

- Before the photo-shoot, practise your smiles and expressions. If you don't like yourself with a full-on cheesy grin then make sure the photographer knows that. Know which side of your face you prefer and how you like to see your smile. When you smile think about something that makes you smile, so that the smile shows in your eyes too.

- Make sure the photographer helps you to achieve flattering poses and gives you ideas on how to sit and stand. Practise in front of a mirror so that you know which poses are best for you.

- Ladies, have your make-up and hair done professionally. The photographer may provide a make-up artist, so use her. Alternatively, visit a make-up counter and have your make-up done there. There is often a fee that is redeemable against product sales. The flash will take away 50 per cent of your make-up so don't be scared if you look more made-up than you are used to.

Enhance your networking with LinkedIn

Now that I've given you some great tips on how to create a stunning Linkedin profile, how can you use it to enhance your networking?

- On returning from a networking event, search for the contacts who you have found and add them to your connections. When inviting someone to connect, add a personal note rather than using the standard message. The person may not remember meeting you at the event or it might be some time before they next log into LinkedIn, so send them a message telling them it was great to meet them at the event and that you would like to stay in touch and look forward to meeting them again soon. If you discussed anything in particular, or spoke about meeting up again then make sure you put that in your message too.

- Do browse through their profile and find out a little more about them. Look through their connections and see if there is anyone else that they know who might be one of your 'big fish' and if relevant you could directly ask them for a referral, or perhaps wait until you get to know them a little better and ask them later.

- When you have some significant news, let your contact list know. If you are running an event, if you win an award or if you do well on a new project, then let your network know. Accompany your broadcast with a request to catch up for a chat soon and you may create a networking spark that invigorates a dead connection.

- Connect with all your old work colleagues. There is something about connecting with people you used to work with that works very well in networking. It's not necessarily about what your past colleagues are doing now, it is about who they know and who they might be able to introduce you to. They will also be interested in who you know, so be prepared to give before you receive!

- Get new connections by joining groups. If you want to work with a particular person or company then look at the groups and discussions that are going on there. Join in the conversation and become a contributor to the group. You must add value before anyone in the group will be prepared to give you a contact or meet you for a face-to-face.

- Track company activity. You can see when someone changes the company they work for in their profile and follow what is going on within a company and view their new hires and leavers. If I were a recruitment consultant I'd be very interested to find out the names of new managers in the areas that I place clients in.

- LinkedIn claims that you will get 40 times more opportunities if your profile is 100 per cent complete. So do complete all your information and keep it up to date. Each change you make is listed in your status, so again you will be 'top of mind' when your colleagues check their news feed.

- Use LinkedIn to do your homework. Before you attend a networking event or an important interview or meeting, research your contacts online if you know who is going to be there. Pay particular attention to mutual connections. Talking about someone you both used to work with is a great way to break the ice.

- Become very active in the Answers section. The more active you are, the more people will read your profile, and the more opportunities you will get.

- Give before you receive. Comment on a colleague's status update. Forward a great job opportunity to a colleague. Connect two colleagues who might be able to do business together. LinkedIn makes all this very easy.

- Support online networking with face-to-face networking. Build foundations online but then meet up for a coffee and build that relationship even further.

 Aha! Moment

My online networking will help me stay connected after events and will also help me to research before events.

Twitter

I personally am not a great tweeter. I have a Twitter account and I use it periodically but I don't find that my target audience hangs out much on Twitter. I get much less response to tweets than I do to Facebook posts, so that's where I spend my online networking time, but you need to test what is best for you.

Twitter is an online social networking service and microblogging service that enables its users to send and read text-based messages of up to 140 characters, known as 'tweets'.

It was launched in July 2006, apparently as a tool to enable journalists to quickly pass information to the media and the masses. In true social media viral strategy, it quickly gained worldwide popularity and now has over

500 million users, generating over 340 million tweets daily and handling over 1.6 billion search queries per day. Twitter has become one of the top ten most visited websites on the Internet.

What do you do on Twitter?

You create an account and send status updates of a maximum of 140 characters. You can use those 140 characters as a link to another article you have written or read, or to direct the user to a picture. You can use #tags (hashtags) as keywords in your message to make it easier for other users to search through your content. A #tag is simply a keyword preceded by a # that groups of users type to identify their subject. I might type "I've just launched a new image course, #8weeks2fabulous. Hope to see you there!" and encourage my followers to use the #tag too.

With Twitter, like Facebook and LinkedIn, you are looking to gather a following and build connections. Join in the conversation with people you respect and subjects you are interested in. As you comment in groups and discussions, other users will follow you and be interested in what you say.

My top tips for Twitter

- Customise your Twitter background. Create an eye-catching background, use a great profile picture and the 160 characters for your bio wisely.

- There are many third-party tools that you can use to post and filter your tweets, including making it easier to manage them on a mobile device. I use Hootsuite to manage and post my tweets. Here are a few other gems:

  - TwitPic. Posts pictures on your tweets. If you want to post pictures while away from the computer, use the Twitterific app.

  - SocialOomph. Twitter tools, including the ability to schedule when a tweet gets posted.

  - Qwitter. I love the name of this one. It is a service that sends an e-mail any time someone unsubscribes from your Twitter profile and mentions a possible post you made that may have triggered their unsubscribe.

- Manageflitter. A fantastic site for managing your followers and getting an easy-to-read overview of people who do not follow you in return, quiet users and inactive users.

- WeFollow. A website that allows you to add yourself to a listing of Twitter users by tags you follow and comment on.

- Tweetbeat. An excellent site that tracks the trending topics on Twitter and gives you a clearer explanation of present and past trending topics.

- Need more inspiration? Search on Google for the latest hot Twitter applications and tools.

- Just like face-to-face networking, listen (or read) more than you tweet. Read the interesting tweets and follow the influential tweeters but only comment when you have something of real value to say. Don't follow everyone and don't expect everyone to follow you. Do Retweet regularly, especially influential tweeters, or people whom you know in person. When you return from a networking event find out if anyone of interest that you met has a Twitter account and follow them.

- Do not whine or complain or say anything defamatory. People will unfollow anyone who does that!

- Understand the terminology. @reply, Direct Message (DM), Follower, Hashtag, Retweet (RT), Trending Topics, and Tweet are just a few.

- Use Twitter search tools to alert you when you or subjects that you are interested in are written about in a tweet.

- Want to see how it is done? Follow the masters (I've listed a few on the following page). These guys really know how to use Twitter to become influential.

- Take your conversation offline as soon as possible. Try to meet face-to-face or move the conversation to e-mail, or you could even pick up the telephone!

- Advertise your Twitter account name on your business card and other social media channels to gain more followers.

- Tweet regularly but don't over tweet — like any other status updates we are not interested in what you had for lunch.

 Fast Fact

Want to learn more about Twitter and see how it should be done? Follow the masters. Here are the top ten tweeters I recommend following:

@GuyKawasaki
@Scobleizer
@jeffbullas
@briansolis
@tonyrobbins
@kevinrose
@timoreilly
@donttrythis
@zappos
@brainpicke

YouTube

Every social media platform that I have spoken about so far could be a book on its own. In fact, there are already many great books on these and many more applications. I just need to mention one more social media platform that the serious networker must have a presence on, or use to research and promote those they would like to network with. YouTube is now the second most popular search engine after Google.

- More than two billion YouTube videos are viewed every day.

- 24 hours of video are uploaded every minute.

- 94 of the world's top advertisers now advertise on YouTube (and we wondered how Google was going to recoup their money when they purchased YouTube for $1.65 billion dollars).

- The number of advertisers using YouTube has increased ten-fold in the last year. This shows how influential this platform is becoming.

Using YouTube to grow your network

If you have your own business, you need a presence on YouTube; perhaps a short video showcasing your products. You could position yourself as an expert in your field by posting some tips online. If you are a little camera-shy, why not get some of your customers to record some testimonials for you. Whatever you decide to do, make sure you have something on YouTube. When someone types in your name or your company name on YouTube, you need to have something come up in the search results, preferably not of you dancing on the bar at last year's Christmas Party!

The importance of social media

We've now looked at Facebook, Pinterest, LinkedIn, Twitter and YouTube, but there are hundreds more platforms that might be right for you. If you underestimate the importance of networking on social media, just look at some of these facts (source: http://en.wikipedia.org/wiki/social_media):

- Social media has overtaken pornography as the number one activity on the web.

- Social networking now accounts for 22 per cent of all time spent online in the US.

- A total of 234 million people age 13 and older in the US used mobile devices in December 2009.

- The number of social media users age 65 and older grew by 100 per cent throughout 2010, so that one in four people in that age group are now part of a social networking site.

Networking effectively on social media actually only requires around 20 minutes a day.

- Over 25 per cent of U.S. Internet page views occurred at one of the top social networking sites in December 2009, up from 13.8 per cent a year before.

- One out of eight couples married in the US last year met via social media, according to statistics released in June 2011.

- One in six higher-education students are enrolled in an online curriculum.

- In June 2011, a US Department of Education study revealed that online students out-performed those receiving face-to-face instruction.

- As of May 2012, Facebook has 901 million users.

- Australia has some of the highest social media usage in the world. In usage of Facebook, Australia ranks highest, with over nine million users spending almost 9 hours per month on the site.

- In June 2011, it was reported that iPhone applications hit one billion in nine months, and Facebook added 100 million users in less than nine months.

- If Facebook was a country it would be the third largest in terms of population — even larger than the US!

- Twitter processed more than one billion tweets in December 2009 and averages almost 40 million tweets per day.

- YouTube is the second largest search engine in the world.

- In four minutes and 26 seconds, 100+ hours of video will be uploaded to YouTube.

Star Tips for social media beyond Facebook

1. Look up special terms in the social media glossary of the 100 most-used terms: http://www.socialbrite.org/sharing-center/glossary/

2. Schedule 15-30 minutes every day to check out what your connections are doing on social media. If possible re-post, re-tweet, share and connect them.

3. Have a brilliant corporate photograph to use on your business social media sites. It's OK for your Facebook one to be more fun and social but definitely not for LinkedIn.

4. Use social media to research contacts you might meet before your networking events or conferences to gain valuable information that can help you to build rapport in conversations.

5. Follow people you meet on their social media platforms.

6. Give before your receive. Connect, share and promote your contacts online, and eventually they will do the same for you.

7. Spend the most time on social media where your target audience and stake-holders are. Research other social media tools that might be of interest to you and watch out for new ones emerging all the time.

8. Have your LinkedIn profile proofread and even possibly professionally written. Check out www.elance.com for professional freelancers who can help you with this.

9. Get out from behind the computer and go and meet people. Online networking supports face-to-face networking. Prior research on social media can make it easier to build rapport face-to-face though.

10. Listen more than you post. Research, repost and promote. Ensure that your social media contributions add value to any conversation.

NETWORKING SUCCESS STORIES

"Friendships are like train journeys. Some people are on for the whole journey and some people are just with you for a few stops. Don't be sad when they get off. Be happy to have enjoyed the ride."

My Auntie Maggy

In this book I've likened networking to dating, with some unwritten rules of what you should and shouldn't do. The nerves, the uncertainty. Am I too forward? Does he like me? Should I call him? Is it too soon? Oh no! He's asked me to meet his parents. What shall I wear? Now we're at the part of the book where you learn to take it slow and send flowers after a great date.

The real networking takes place outside of networking events. It's the effort you put in afterwards to stay in touch and follow up that will pay dividends. Social media makes this so much easier, but you still have to make a conscious effort to keep in touch and stay connected. It can sometimes take years for a relationship to develop, and you'll often find that you don't end up with the outcome you had hoped for at the beginning. Then again, sometimes you end up with more than you could ever have expected.

Fast Fact

More than anything else, you need to listen out for opportunities for others and give more than you receive.

In this chapter, I will give you some examples of how networking has worked for me on a personal and business level. As you read these stories, notice how long it often takes to reap the benefits from a relationship, and how the outcomes could not have possibly been predicted at the first meeting.

Success story #1

She Plc is the name of a fabulous women's networking lunch formerly hosted by the Thames Valley Chamber of Commerce and run by Mary Flavelle. Mary always sourced fabulous venues for her luncheons, and this month we were lunching in the amazing Penny Hill Park in the Surrey countryside. Pennyhill Park is an exclusive members golf club. Lunch there would normally be quite expensive and it's the sort of place you would go for a very special occasion. Because of this, the event attracted a large crowd of businesswomen eager to put on their posh frocks and check out the exclusive venue.

Aha! Moment

If I hold an event in an exclusive location, people will attend just because they want to check out the venue.

I arrive at the venue early, wearing one of my very posh frocks, greet the host and ask her if she needs any help with the preparation.

I look through the guest list, making a mental note of the names that I know. There are some names that I recognise but I can't quite recall so I quickly check the contact details on my phone. I see their picture and a few notes that I jotted down at a previous event so I will be able to recognise them, greet them by name and recall any important information about them.

Fast Fact

It's a good idea to arrive early at the venue, then you can talk to the host before she gets too busy with guests. Helping her with the preparation is very smart, as she will probably go out of her way to help you in the future.

Aha! Moment

If I store details about someone in my contacts and then synchronise my contacts with my phone, I can easily gain access to pictures and personal information in seconds by simply searching for their name on my phone.

I look through the list of contacts for the people I don't know and scan their company names and job titles. I'm looking through the list trying to establish which guests could be big fishes and tick the names of the people that I am most interested in meeting. You will not always have the luxury of a guest list, but if you do then make sure that you use it before and after the event, as it can save you a lot of administration.

Guests start arriving; Mary is greeting them and signing them in. I go and talk to Cheryl who has just arrived. I met Cheryl at an event about a year ago — she became my client, I hired her as a photographer, and subsequently recommended her to a few of my clients as well as business colleagues. Cheryl and I are now great friends. After a little bit of chit chat, I ask Cheryl if she has previously met any of the names that I have ticked as my big fish. I find that Cheryl knows two of the people that I am interested in meeting, so I ask her if she would be kind enough to make an introduction when she sees them. I ask Cheryl if she is looking to catch up with anyone on her list that I might know. She points out one contact that I know, and I make a note to ensure that I introduce this lady to Cheryl later.

Aha! Moment

People that I know may already be connected to people that I want to meet, so I can use them to connect.

Cheryl and I move away from the registration desk so the area does not become too congested. We move close to the drinks table so that we can easily connect with people who are coming to pick up their glass of wine. I spot someone walking in on her own looking quite nervous. "Drinks are over here," I say, "Would you like red or white wine?" "White," she replies, and I hand her a glass. "Hi, I'm Sharon Connolly," I say as I smile and shake her hand. "Alison Crook," she replies. "And this is Cheryl Bradley. Cheryl is an amazing photographer who I have been privileged to work with on a number of occasions."

 Aha! Moment

It looks really great when I promote my friends and colleagues when networking. They look good, and I seem more charming and gracious.

Cheryl and Alison shake hands, and I ask Alison what she does. Alison has a fascinating business. She has a limousine coach. It's a coach that has been completely remodelled, and she describes it as a private jet on wheels. She rents the coach out to celebrities, and to organisations for corporate events. As Cheryl and I chat with Alison, we learn that the coach is new and that she is new to networking, and more than anything else she is finding it difficult to work from home all day without other people in the office to motivate her. We learn that she has two teenage children, she used to live in Devon, she has a boat and enjoys sailing at the weekends. We find out that she is currently living in a bit of a disaster zone at home as her husband is building a new kitchen. Steve has a job in air conditioning, but he also drives the coach on weekends.

Alison is a tiddler for me. Initially there is no direct synergy between our businesses. She looks great, so she doesn't need an image consultant, and I am not currently in a position to hire a luxury coach.

What happened next?

A few years later, Alison hired me to train her in presentation skills when making some corporate videos to promote her flourishing business. I styled her teenage daughter for her prom. As Alison became more confident at networking, she grew her circle of contacts and became a leader at one of my LadiesWhoLatte networking groups. Because of her connections to some great venues in the area, Alison gets me invited to some very swanky exclusive events. Alison became a presenter on local radio and I was invited regularly to the show to talk about fashion. I referred a couple of corporate clients to Alison who have hired her coach. Alison also donated the coach for a day to raise money for a charity that I work with.

Success story #2

Back to the same networking event: Cheryl and I are chatting with Alison when another lady enters the room looking a little lost. Standing close to the drinks table, I get her a drink and do the introductions. Having listened carefully to what Alison does, I'm able to introduce her to the new lady with panache. "Deborah, this is Alison Crook. Like you, this is her first event. Deborah, Alison has this most amazing business. She hires out a bus that looks like private jet inside. And this is Cheryl Bradley, an amazing photographer who I have worked with often. What do you do, Deborah?"

 Aha! Moment

If I introduce contacts, I get to practise their names more to help me commit them to memory, and new contacts will feel valued as they know I have listened to what they do.

Deborah introduces herself and explains that she makes bespoke wedding stationery. She shows us some samples of her work, which is stunning. Cheryl occasionally does wedding photography, so she and Deborah have a synergy, and Alison's coach is sometimes used for weddings so the little group start chatting enthusiastically. We also learn that Deborah has a three-year-old son and lives very close to me. She's been looking to join a new gym so I offer to get her a guest pass at my gym so she can try it out.

What happened next?

Deborah and Cheryl went on to do lots of work together in the wedding industry. Both Cheryl and I ordered bespoke Christmas cards to send to our best clients. Deborah created some beautiful gift vouchers for my image business. When I met her, Deborah was recently divorced and her confidence was at an all-time low. She was very scared of going out dating again and lacked confidence in presenting her business. She hired me for an image consultation, and her confidence was hugely increased. Deborah turned into an absolute firecracker. Her stationery business grew from strength to strength, and many adoring men were lining up to wine and dine her.

A year later, Deborah organised a huge charity breast cancer event. I was the guest speaker, giving a talk on fashion and looking good. Someone in the audience worked at the British Heart Foundation and they hired me for many workshops over the next few years. Cheryl offered a lifestyle photoshoot as a raffle prize, and the family who won the photoshoot loved it so much that they bought an additional £3,000 worth of prints, and they referred Cheryl to many friends. Alison helped Deborah to secure a great deal on the venue and publicised her event on her radio show, helping her to sell more tickets and raise even more money.

Alison, Cheryl and Deborah are real people. The connections that I wrote about really took place over a number of years, and you will find all of these contacts on my Facebook page as friends and business colleagues.

Deborah moved out of the area and, inspired by Cheryl's photography, she took some classes and is now a professional photographer. Alison sold the coach but she still works with the new owners and gets a commission on each client she refers. Alison now runs an event management company as well as her radio show. Mary Flavelle, the organiser of the She Plc lunch, frequently stands in for Alison on the radio show.

In this story, the relationships and successful business deals took time to nurture. How could I have known that meeting a lady who makes stationery could have led to me getting a client that paid me to deliver monthly training courses for over five years? How could Deborah know that seven years after that event, she would love working as a professional photographer? I have many stories like these and many more in the making with my networking relationships still being nurtured daily.

The fruits of your networking will often take years to ripen. Sow seeds and nurture relationships. You never know where they will end up.

How does your garden grow?

Let me point out a few of the key things that helped me make these relationships work.

At the start of the story I knew Cheryl. Cheryl was one of my very early clients when I had just trained as an image consultant. Her sister had bought her a voucher for a make-up lesson. These vouchers cost just £20. Cheryl came to visit me and I spent over two hours with her explaining different looks, products and applications. It was supposed to be a 30-minute session taster session but I went above and beyond this. I was learning my new craft and delighted to have a client lapping up the information. Cheryl then went onto my mailing list and began to receive my regular newsletters.

Fast Fact

It's easier to get repeat business or referrals from existing clients than to generate new ones, so do stay in contact with all your clients regularly.

Six months later, Cheryl came to an event I was holding in my home to promote the new season's fashions. In Chapter 6, I mentioned an event that I hold in department stores with hundreds of guests. This event started out with just four ladies sitting on my sofa and Cheryl was one of them. Cheryl paid £10 for that ticket and received hours of information.

When Cheryl and her husband Andrew started their photography business a year later, they both hired me for a full consultation to help with their personal brands. This included branding, image, networking and personal shopping. They were my biggest client at that time. After our successful shopping trip, I suggested that we celebrate with a glass of wine, over which our friendship was sealed. Andrew later worked for me as a freelance IT training consultant.

Fast Fact

Cheryl saw that I was a generous and giving person who was passionate about what I did. By attending events and staying in touch with her over a couple of years, she trusted me and I was her first choice for her personal branding session.

Another pivotal point in this relationship building was between myself and Deborah Lee. Through our small talk I learnt that she lived close to me and was looking for a gym to join. I got her a free session at my gym, which she liked and joined. I received two lovely white fluffy dressing gowns and a bottle of champagne for referring a new member. I shared the champagne with Deborah. We often met at the gym for coffee. They had a great playroom there for her three-year-old so we could sit and talk while Ben played happily. Deborah talked about her lack of confidence so I gave her lots of free tips on how to get more confident through the way she dressed. Each little tip helped her, so she decided to book a full image session with me. After seeing me speak at networking events, she felt confident enough to ask me to deliver a talk for her prestigious charity event.

For both Cheryl and me, speaking at networking events was also a key to our success. We teamed up and ran a lunch-time session called 'How to look good in photographs'. We travelled around giving this talk at many women's lunches. I would talk about what to wear to look fabulous and Cheryl would talk about how to stand, sit and pose to look amazing in photographs. I often use the tips that I learnt from her in my work now, and I now collaborate with other photographers here in Singapore to give similar workshops.

Aha! Moment

If I speak at an event, everyone present will get to know who I am and what I do. I may also be able to obtain all the email addresses of the guests so that I can connect with them afterwards.

Not all relationships are as easily forged as the ones that I have mentioned. They may take a lot more time and effort. One important thing to remember if you want to be really effective at networking is to keep great records. You can use a fancy CRM system, or I just use my Outlook contacts. I write notes about the person, both business and personal, so that I can remember their details.

Fast Fact

Add a photograph to your Outlook or Gmail contact. You will see their picture if they send you an email, and depending on your technology this will link to your smart phone so that you have access to it on the move.

Aha! Moment

At a networking event I can check details of someone I previously met and have forgotten details about.

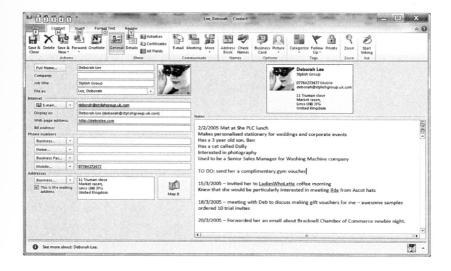

Danger Zone

If you write details like this on the contact card then be careful not to forward that contact via your smart phone or email system. If you have detailed that they have a big nose and yellow teeth, it could cause you a few problems!

Depending on how many contacts you have, you may not want to add every contact into your contact system. You should definitely add details of your big fish, but not everyone. Sometimes I come back from a networking event with over 30 business cards — what are you going to do with all your business cards? It's not practical to add them all in and write lots of details about them, but I do need to record and categorise them. Big fish go in my Outlook contacts and I connect to them on LinkedIn. Tiddlers and old boots go into a spreadsheet of contacts and into my CRM system so they receive a copy of my newsletters and forthcoming events. When they receive the first newsletter I include a paragraph saying that they have received the newsletter because they met me at a recent networking event. The CRM system handles unsubscribes, so if they wish to opt out of the list then this is easily managed.

 Danger Zone

When you add contacts into your CRM system or similar then make sure you keep a record of when and where you met them. Some CRM systems can freeze your account if they receive complaints that you are spamming. Keep the business cards as proof that you did actually meet this person rather than buying a mailing list. When you swap business cards, ask for permission to add them to your mailing list.

The importance of referrals

My final contribution to your world domination via networking is a few words of advice on getting referrals. I believe that the most important connection may not be between you and the person that you are talking to, but rather it will be between you and who they can refer you to in their network. So remember that referral is a very important part of networking. I often hear people add a request for a referral in their elevator pitch. For example:

> "Hi my name is Sharon Connolly and I'm an image consultant, if you know anyone who needs help with their image perhaps you could pass on my details."

I hear this a lot but it is ineffective. Firstly, in order for someone to refer you they will have to trust that you can do a good job. Before someone gives me a referral for an image session they need to have seen evidence of other make-overs that I have done, or perhaps they will need to see me present to realise that I really am an authority on my subject.

When you do find yourself in a position to ask for a referral, perhaps at the end of a talk that you have given, be very specific about the type of referral you are looking for. This, for example, is not good:

> "Thank you for taking the time to listen to my presentation. If you know anyone who needs help with their image, please pass on my details."

Try something like this instead:

> "Thank you for taking the time to listen to my presentation, I hope you enjoyed it and I welcome your feedback. Do you know anyone who could benefit from my advice? My typical client is a lady aged between 35 and 45 who has lost confidence in dressing and experimenting with clothes. She is still really attractive but she just seems to be hiding herself away under drab clothes and wearing the same old thing again and again. If you know anyone who needs help to get their light to shine again I'd love to invite them to one of my free talks so I would be happy if you could connect us."

Note that I was very specific about the type of client that I would like referring to. As I'm describing that lady, people are mentally scanning through their friends, family and business network trying to identify that exact person in their network. When they think of her, they really connect with what I'm saying and can see how I could really help this person. I am much more likely to get a referral by being very specific about who I would like to work with.

Myth Buster

By being very specific like this, aren't you cutting out the possibility of other clients?

No, I don't think so. When I have described my ideal client then I'll often get asked if I deal with men or teenagers as well. Being specific will hone in on contacts in your listeners' mental database, but it rarely excludes others too.

Be very clear from the outset about referral fees. Some contacts will expect financial compensation if they refer a client to you. I think that is totally acceptable. If someone is in a position to pass you lucrative business leads without you being able to reciprocate, then there should be financial compensation. The most important thing is that you are clear about the relationship from the start.

Star Tips for being a star in your own networking success stories

1. See every contact as a potential networking connection. You never know where it may lead.

2. Hone your listening skills and pay attention so that you can find out as much information about people as possible and then look out for any opportunity that may benefit them.

3. Keep records of your contacts. A pile of business cards in a box is not useful. Add them to a database and categorise them. Be sure to keep in contact with your big fishes.

4. Connect to your big fish on social media, particularly LinkedIn.

5. Revisit and review your inner circle of friends often. It's easy to miss opportunities for connections and referrals with the people closest to us. Make sure that everyone in your social circle knows what opportunities you are looking for and vice versa.

6. Stay 'top of mind'. You must be visible to your network. Think of ways you can pop up on their radar. Attend events, send them a newsletter, write for a magazine, speak on the radio. For people to help you, they must not forget about you.

7. Be proactive. If there are no suitable networking events in your area or networking groups in your organisation, then start one. Don't whine about it and wait for someone else to do it. Get out there and create the opportunities.

8. Contribute to all the groups you belong to. Online and offline, do what you can to be more visible to your network. Raise your profile by volunteering to be a speaker, or joining the committee or organising team.

9. Have fun networking. Treat each event like you are going to a party. Get dressed up, be enthusiastic and attend with the mindset that you will be mixing and mingling with interesting people and great friends.

10. Remember, opportunities are never lost. Someone else will take the one you missed.

INDEX

ABOUT THE AUTHOR

Sharon Connolly lives by the beach in Singapore with her chocolate Labrador, Poppy. She's rarely standing still, and if she's not working, she's running, skating, cycling, singing, dancing, skiing or socialising.

An international authority on professional image, Sharon is originally from the UK. Through more than 20 years of running her own businesses, Sharon has created most of her opportunities from networking and referrals. She put her networking know-how to good use when she relocated to Singapore in 2010 and rapidly became a well-known speaker and trainer. Sharon now delivers one-to-one coaching and group training on the importance of how to create an impactful first impression with a powerful image. Her clients range from stay-at-home mums to CEOs of global organisations.

Sharon is the founder of the global women's networking group, LadiesWhoLatte, which runs over 40 meetings every month and helps women grow their businesses and gain confidence.

Prior to training to be an image consultant, Sharon spent 15 years working in IT. Her technical know-how meant that she quickly grasped the new technologies of social media marketing and was able to assist many of her SME clients to easily do the same.

Success Skills Series

STTS Training (previously ST Training Solutions), based in Singapore, offers a wide range of popular, practical training programmes conducted by experienced, professional trainers. As CEO, Shirley Taylor takes a personal interest in working closely with trainers to ensure that each workshop is full of valuable tools, helpful guidelines and powerful action steps that will ensure a true learning experience for all participants. Some of the workshops offered are:

Powerful Business Writing Skills
Energise your E-mail Writing Skills
Success Skills for Secretaries and Support Staff
Communication: Your Key to Success
Assetive Communication Skills
Powerful Presentation Skills
Better Business Communication
Speaking With Confidence
Emotional Intelligence at Work
Powerful Negotiating
Power-Packed Productivity
Dealing with Difficult People and Situations
Microsoft Office Productivity Buffet

Shirley Taylor is also host of a very popular annual conference called ASSAP — the Asian Summit for Secretaries and Admin Professionals — organised in April each year by STTS Training.

Find out more about STTS Training at www.sttstraining.com. Visit www.shirleytaylor.com for additional resources.